WARNING:

Put this book right back on the shelf if...

A. You are a guy. (This book is for women only.)
B. You're a Christian, and you don't think Christians should read books about sex.
C. You are a married woman who has *never once* been too busy, tired, irritated, hurt, uninterested, upset, or selfish to cheerfully make love to her husband.
D. You are too embarrassed to take it up to the counter and buy it.

On second thought...

- If you're a married man and this book's title has intrigued you, buy it for your wife. (You can sneak peeks when she's not paying attention.)
- If you're one who thinks sexual enjoyment is not for Christians, maybe you *should* read this book. You just might have a change of heart.
- If you're shy about buying, do it just this once.
- Oh, yeah—and if you fit in category C...you're a fibber. You'd better get the book.

Is That All He Thinks About?

Marla Taviano

HARVEST HOUSE PUBLISHERS

EUGENE, OREGON

Cover by Garborg Design Works, Savage, Minnesota

Cover photo © Itstock / Inmagine

IS THAT ALL HE THINKS ABOUT?
Copyright © 2007 by Marla Taviano
Published by Harvest House Publishers
Eugene, Oregon 97402
www.harvesthousepublishers.com

Library of Congress Cataloging-in-Publication Data
   Taviano, Marla, 1975-
    Is that all he thinks about? / Marla Taviano.
       p. cm.
    ISBN-13: 978-0-7369-1898-5 (pbk.)
    ISBN-10: 0-7369-1898-1 (pbk.)
    1. Sex—Religious aspects—Christianity. 2. Men—Psychology. I. Title.
    BT708.T38 2007
    248.8'435—dc22   2006021725

Printed in the United States of America

07 08 09 10 11 12 13 14 15 / BP-CF / 10 9 8 7 6 5 4 3 2 1

To Gabe,
my very best friend.
You're all I could ever want—
in the bedroom and out.

And to our parents—
Ron and Chris, and Rock and Janelle.
Thirty-plus years of marriage
and the passion still burns!
You guys are our heroes!

Acknowledgments

A big hug and thank-you to all the brave and honest gals who filled out surveys or chatted with me personally. (Names have been changed and details disguised.) Your stories will undoubtedly touch many lives.

CONTENTS

What's In It for Me?

Maybe you've read a slew of books about sex. If so, you probably want a guarantee that if you decide to read *this* one, it won't end up sounding exactly the same as the last five.

I'm not going to sit here and make empty promises.

Will you learn something new every paragraph? Mmm…possibly. Will you laugh out loud at least two or three times a chapter? Umm…it depends. Will you have an "aha!" moment that inspires you to a bigger and better life? Hmm…hard to say.

By now you may be asking, *So why should I read this book, for crying out loud?*

Because you want the sex you share with your husband to be sweeter.

Now, this is not an exhaustive how-to manual, by any stretch, but I think you'll pick up a helpful tip or two throughout these pages.

This *is* a feel-good, sometimes-laugh-out-loud sort of book. More important, this book is based on a Christian worldview, not watered down or sugar-coated. I have also tried to strike a balance—straightforward but not sensational. My prayer from the outset was that I would be sensitive to God's leading as I wrote.

I do have lofty ideals for this book. I'd love for you to finish the last page, take a deep sigh, and say, "This is the first day of the rest of my marriage." I would love for you to forever see your husband, your marriage, our world and culture, with new eyes—and approach life with a new attitude.

Too bad life is not as simple as reading a book and—voilà—instant marriage makeover! But books can definitely impact lives, and I do believe the Spirit of God can speak directly to your heart through my puny, human words (and the words I've borrowed directly from Him).

Some parts might make you laugh, some will make you squirm, some will make you stop and think—and hopefully, some will make you stand up and take action. My hope is that, when all is said and done, you will walk away changed. And your marriage will be blessed.

And that is also my fervent prayer.

Let's Chat

Why did I write this book?

Well, to be honest, God had made it clear to me that my sex life needed a boost. To *write* about sex, I knew I'd have to *read* about it and *think* about it—two things that have proven to increase my sexual desire. My husband would be the recipient of a sexual double whammy. (No complaints from him, I might add.)

A lot of times, sad to say, my writing *detracts* from my libido. After a long day, the kids are finally in bed, and I want to sit and write until I collapse onto my own bed in exhaustion. I just can't work sex in (or so I say).

So, in an effort to please my husband *and* get my daily writing fix, why not combine work and pleasure and write a book about sex?

"Doesn't your husband feel like you're *using* him?" you want to know. Well, no, he doesn't. In fact, he'd like me to use him a lot more often.

He actually can't quit grinning about the whole idea. He has just one stipulation. "You can use me as a guinea pig for your 'research,'" he says, "as long as the experiments continue when the book is done!"

He also likes the whole tax write-off idea. You know, since I'm writing a book about sex, I can legitimately spend tax-free dollars on research materials. (I'll make a note to check the tax laws. I'd hate to try explaining to my accountant why "whipped cream" and "edible panties" showed up as business expenses in my tax records for this year.)

When my friends and family first heard the title of my previous book *(From Blushing Bride to Wedded Wife)*, they often jumped to an incorrect conclusion—that my choice of subject matter must mean I viewed myself as an expert on the topic of marriage.

Then they read the book.

They soon realized that the recurring theme throughout my writing is this: "If I must boast I will boast of the things that show my weakness."*

So, now that I've written a book about sex, am I a self-proclaimed sex expert with a to-die-for sex life? Or will I again be writing about my struggles and weaknesses in a particular area of my life?

Just start reading chapter 1, and it won't take you long to figure it out.

As I write, I remind myself, "Cover this in prayer. Ask God to humble you. There's really no guarantee anyone will even buy, let alone *like,* your book. It's fine to share truth in a fun way, but without His help and blessing, lives will never be affected or changed." And so I have committed to pray for this book from its inception to its publication and beyond. And many other women are praying as well.

And while I'm in prayer mode, I'm praying for my own sex life, too—for a better attitude, more desire, more energy, more unselfishness—because I'm realizing more each day that I need God's help to make this work. Many days I find it much easier to sit down at my desk and *write* about sex than go upstairs and *have* it.

We're in This Together, Sister

You and I are a lot alike. Though I can't speak for you completely, if it were up to me, I'd put my own needs and desires first 100 percent of the

* 2 Corinthians 11:30.

time. I love the Lord, I love my husband…but I struggle with selfishness, a lack of sexual desire, and making sex a priority in my busy life.

God tells us in the Bible that sex is a requirement for married people—not an optional activity. But He never suggests it should be given begrudgingly, out of a sense of duty. In fact, He seems to think it is something incredible—a delightful act that can bring us loads of pleasure as long as we both shall live. Wow.

Most of you don't have the luxury of writing about sex for a living. But you can *read* about it, and that's part of the reason I wrote this book. Just reading it will help enhance your desire and breathe new life into your relationship with your husband. And if you take it a step further and *act* on what you've read—then *wow!*

We're not talking about a walk in the park here—it's more like a hike. You're gonna sweat a bit. Your muscles are gonna ache a little. But the good news is, we're going to journey together, supporting each other every step of the way. And when we get to the top, the view will be glorious!

Let's go, girl!

A
FRESH
PERSPECTIVE

Chapter 1

The "Conditions for Sex" List

At one point last year, my husband and I were struggling in the bedroom. I was less than thrilled about making love. He wanted to know why I wasn't in the mood.

"What can I do to make you want sex more?" he asked.

Ahh…the very question I'd been waiting for. Just the encouragement I needed to pull The List out of my pocket, unfold it, and begin to read.

"It's a proven fact that, for women, sex doesn't start in the bedroom. I need to feel loved and cherished all day long. You can't just go about your business, neglect my needs and desires, and then expect me to make passionate love to you. You want me to want you? Here's what you need to do."

I ignored the blank look in his eyes—he had already begun to tune me out—and kept going.

"First of all, you can get up bright and early (before the sun) and spend time with God in His Word and prayer. I'm sure you realize you haven't exactly been a spiritual leader lately.

"Then you can wake me up with a nice little back scratch and help the girls with their breakfast while I linger in bed for an extra 20 minutes or so.

"Since you're working from home now, I'd like to see you putting in a lot of hours—even overtime—so I can have a little extra cash to spend frivolously.

"If I need you to help me out with the kids during the day (and I will), I want you to do it willingly and happily. It'd be even better if you could anticipate my needs without me having to verbalize them. When the girls are fighting upstairs and I'm busy at my computer, that would be a good time for you to step in (hint, hint). I'm sure whatever you're doing at the time can wait.

"Little love notes on the mirror, a bouquet of roses delivered to the door every now and again (once a week is plenty), sweet kisses—offers to do the dishes, vacuum the living room, make dinner—all of those would help get me in the mood. Did I leave anything out?

"Basically, Gabe, you need to understand that if you want sex, you've got to meet my emotional needs first. Any questions?"

<hr />

Okay, so maybe I'm exaggerating a little, but we had different versions of this discussion about five or six times over the course of a few months. I'll bet you're curious about Gabe's reaction.

Well, it varied. One time he felt defeated and hopeless. Once he got really angry. One time he just threw up his hands and threw in the towel. Once he accused me of being selfish.

"*Me? Selfish?*" I was appalled. "You're the one who wants me to make mad love to you every other night of the week while you just sit there and contribute *nothing* to our emotional relationship during the day! And you think *I'm* selfish?"

Well, I never! Since Gabe obviously didn't give two hoots about my womanly needs, I decided to take them to God in prayer. (Now that's a concept.)

"God," I said, "we have a problem. Correction. *Gabe* has a problem.

He wants sex—lots of sex—with no strings attached. He wants what he wants, and he's not willing to meet my needs first. And then, get this—he has the nerve to call *me* selfish!"

I asked God nicely to please bring about some positive (and much-needed) changes in my husband. And quickly.

Guess what He did instead. The unthinkable and illogical. Not only did He not take my side against Gabe, but He knocked me upside the head with conviction. He told me in that no-nonsense way of His that I was way off base when I expected Gabe to hold up his end of "the bargain" (as *I* defined it) before I would meet his sexual needs.

I slowly began to realize I was holding Gabe hostage to a million-and-one "if-then" statements. "*If* you do this, *then* I'll do that." This was conditional love at its worst. I was guilty of loving with a thousand strings attached.

Is That What You *Really* Want?

I once had a woman say to me, "I didn't get married just to spend my days making some guy happy." After talking with her for awhile, it became apparent that what she had in mind was more along the lines of marrying a guy whose goal was to spend *his* days making *her* happy.

So many women get married dreaming of nothing more than themselves and their own selfish desires. I was one of those women, thinking about all I could *get*, not what I could *give*.

We put so little emphasis on giving, in fact, that we sabotage our marriages. Whatever happened to "do nothing out of selfish ambition" or "look not only to your own interests but also to the interests of others"—phrases we find in Philippians 2?

Regardless of how marvelous it might sound, we don't *really* want a relationship that is all take and no give. A selfish relationship can never truly fulfill us. God has created us in such a way that we only find true, lasting joy when we give of ourselves to others.

And besides, where are you going to find a guy who would actually be willing to devote his entire life to satisfying your every whim? Even if you found the most godly, unselfish guy on the planet, he's probably looking for a gal a little more like himself. A fellow giver, not a self-centered moocher like you or me.

Attitude Check

My friend Mary Ann jokes that her husband Dan's all-time favorite Bible verse is 1 Corinthians 7:4—"The wife's body does not belong to her alone but also to her husband." It sure isn't politically correct, I'll give it that. But then again, PC isn't exactly the apostle Paul's middle name (or his initials).

The Message paraphrase puts a neat little twist on it.

> The marriage bed must be a place of mutuality—the husband seeking to satisfy his wife, the wife seeking to satisfy her husband. Marriage is not a place to "stand up for your rights." Marriage is a decision to serve the other, whether in bed or out.

According to Paul, sex is more than something you do or don't do as you feel like it. It's an explicit command from our Creator.

You may wonder what credibility a single guy like Paul has when it comes to marital sex. Well, at least we know he wasn't writing this stuff just to guilt-trip his wife into bed with him. And he's as credible as they come, because Paul's "book contracts" came straight from God Himself.

If God commands me to have sex with my husband and I don't want to, does that mean I have a rebellious—a sinful—attitude? I'm not fond of that idea.

If I have low sexual desire, I'd rather just blame it on my personality or my femininity or something. "You know, that's just the way God made me."

Or better yet, I could blame it on my husband. "He certainly doesn't help matters. If he'd actually make an effort at showing he cares about me, I might want to have sex more often."

Okay, girls, I'm going to get right to the heart of the matter, cut straight to the gut of this book. I have a proposition. Are you sitting down?

Here it goes: *I propose that you and I take a great big step and commit to no more blame-shifting. No more excuses. No more pointing fingers. It's high time we took responsibility for something that has been entrusted to us by God. Making love to our husbands. Often. With a good attitude.* Are you up to the challenge? And ready for some fun?

I am a woman just like you. I don't *need* sex all that often. And because of that, I have a hard time understanding how my husband's requests for sex stem from a deep physical and emotional need, not just a selfish desire.

According to God, whether we want to or not is not the issue. Sex isn't optional. It's not debatable. It's not an elective. It's a required course.

"The frequency of sex depends on the other person's need, not ours alone," Stormie Omartian says in *The Power of a Praying Wife*. "If your attitude about having sex comes down to only what you need or what you don't want, then you don't have God's perspective."

Oh, there are plenty of "good" reasons. I'm too busy. My children are a full-time job. I'm overwhelmed by life. My husband has hurt me emotionally. He has a terrible habit he just won't give up. I've lost that lovin' feelin'...

Lots of reasons why we don't want to have sex, but the Bible says that spending time in prayer is the only valid reason for abstinence.* And I don't know about you, but my extensive prayer life isn't usually on my list of excuses.

You're His Only Hope

"Why should I have to have sex when I don't feel like it?" asks my friend Claire. "If I'm not in the mood, I think it's selfish of him to ask."

The problem for Claire's husband is that Claire is *never* in the mood. And Claire is not abnormal, as I'm sure many of you would attest to. "I think I need to take some kind of pill or something," she told me, "because I just don't care if I ever have sex."

But it's not all about "What can I do to want sex more?" That's only part of it. The bigger issue is this—feelings or no, do it with a good attitude. God will let the desire follow. Maybe not right away, but it will come.

---

* See 1 Corinthians 7:5.

God says, "Obey me when you don't feel like it—when you can't see the final outcome—and I'll make it worth your while."

My friend Arin recently shared that she was completely uninterested in sex.

"So, what do you love?" I asked her. "And be honest. You don't have to tell me you love reading your Bible and being a mom."

"Scrapbooking, shopping, and eating at nice restaurants," she said without hesitation.

"What if you could only do those things if Jeff were willing to do them with you?" I asked her.

A Question of Neglect

Stormie Omartian shares some great wisdom. She explains that sex is pure need for men, and when this crucial part of him is neglected, it's hard for him to even see what you need.

"Wives sometimes have it backward," Stormie says. "We can have sex after we get these other issues settled. But actually there is a far greater chance of settling the other issues if sex comes first...Whether all conditions are perfect or whether you feel like it or not isn't the point."

I know I've had it backward many a time. I thought Gabe was selfish for not meeting my needs first. Yet how is that any different from me not meeting his first?

Radio talk-show host Dr. Laura Schlessinger takes the selfish idea a bit further. She boldly asserts (and I agree) that refusing sex with your husband is the "moral equivalent of infidelity." A shocking statement maybe, but it makes sense.

"Intentionally depriving a spouse of his legitimate needs," she says, "stems from being unfaithful to the intent of the vows."

No, you probably didn't say, "I promise to have sex with you at least three times a week as long as we both shall live" in front of the church on your wedding day. But you did vow to love, honor, and cherish your husband—and sex is a huge part of that.

"That's stupid," she told me without batting an eye.

"Go with me here, girl. I have a point."

"Okay," she said, playing along. "I'd never get to scrapbook, I'd hardly ever shop, and we'd eat out once or twice a month. But we'd never go to my favorite two restaurants, because he insists he doesn't like them."

"So, let me ask you this—since your husband doesn't enjoy scrapbooking, shopping, or eating out at nice restaurants on a frequent basis, do you go without these things?"

"Of course not. That's what my girlfriends are for."

"Hmm…okay. Let me get this straight. You like scrapbooking, but not sex. He likes sex, but not scrapbooking. Correct?"

"Uh, yes."

"When you refuse to have sex with him, who does he call to satisfy that craving?"

"He better not be calling anybody!"

"Why not? You do."

"Not for sex!"

"Right, but sex is not *your* deepest need. So, while you're getting your deepest needs and desires met, your husband is going without. It's perfectly acceptable for other people to meet these needs for you, but you are the only person on the face of this earth he is allowed to go to for sex."

"You can't tell me that sex is a *need. I* don't need it."

"Oh, boy—if I had a 'wrong answer' buzzer, you'd so be getting buzzed right now, girl. But I don't. So let's not even discuss whether sex is a real need for a man or not. Let's talk about scrapbooking. Need or want?"

"Okay, so it's not a need, but I think the real solution here is for my husband to find a hobby he can do without me. Maybe that would take his mind off sex."

"Is that how you visualize your ideal marriage—you going off and doing your thing, him going off and doing his? Two separate people going in two separate directions? Why even bother getting married? We can't use our differences as an excuse to avoid doing something our husbands want to do. And besides, sex is not just a *hobby* for your husband. Taking his *mind* off it isn't the answer."

Our conversation continued…round and round, going absolutely nowhere. My powers of persuasion seemed to have no effect. So I did the wise thing. I stopped talking and asked God to help her see the light. (The verdict is still out.)

Your husband agreed to marry you with his sex drive intact, fully aware he would be entirely dependent on you to meet all his sexual needs. If, for some reason, you were unable or unwilling to meet those needs, he understood they would go unmet. Saying "I do" to you included placing his sexual needs and identity out on the table—naked and vulnerable—for you to do with as you please.

According to God, I am the only one allowed to meet my husband's sexual desires. An awesome responsibility, yes, but what a privilege.

Making Time for Making Love

I'm a list-maker, a go-getter, a type A, a Martha, a busybody. Call me what you will. So much to do, so little time.

Sure, sex is on my to-do list. Somewhere, I think. It's just not close enough to the top to make it into my day most of the time.

If we're honest with ourselves, we'll admit we can always make time for the things we really want to do. It's all about choices. What do I choose to do with the 24 hours I'm given each day?

Picture this: On my desk I have two piles. One is a stack of bills to pay and papers to file. The other "pile" has just one item in it—the latest Christian chick-lit novel by my favorite author.

I have one hour available. If I pick up the book and say, "I just don't have time to pay the bills today," am I being truthful?

And when I say, "I'd love to have sex more often, but I'm just too busy," am I being truthful? Making time for sex doesn't depend so much on my schedule and circumstances as it does on my attitude.

Now, of course you don't *have* the time (especially if you have kids), and you probably won't *find* the time to do it either. You have to *make* time for sex.

What things are robbing you of time that could be spent with your husband? Television? Novels and magazines? Your cell phone? The computer? Your writing career? (Ahem.) When these choices interfere with intimacy with our spouse, we're being selfish and foolish, plain and simple.

I have come to realize something amazing. So amazing, in fact, that there's not a chance you'll believe me until you try it. Sex takes time, yes, but when I'm having it regularly, I actually get more done. Life runs more smoothly. I have a calming sense of peace and happiness. Honestly and truly—I am not making this up.

That's not an accident. It's the way God works.

It's like the object lesson with the Mason jar, the golf balls and the gravel. If I put the gravel in first, the golf balls won't fit. But if I put the golf balls in the jar first, then the gravel fits nicely all around it. Same with sex. When I make time to make love like God commands me to do, He'll take care of all the other stuff. He really will. I just have to trust Him enough to put everything aside and have sex.

The bottom line is, we can always make time for the things (and people) that are most important to us. Make it your goal to show your husband you love him by giving him nice-sized chunks of your valuable time.

Coming into Your Own—God's Way

We're starting to understand what we need to do. But it's much easier said than done. Changing our attitudes is not a simple, clear-cut process. In fact, it can get downright messy.

But God promises that when we seek Him *first*, everything else will be given to us as well. When we pray, "Change *my* heart—don't worry about *him*," everything else will fall into place.

Instead of asking, "What will bring me happiness and fulfillment?" ask, "How can I satisfy and complete my husband?"

Instead of looking at sex through the lens of our own perceptions, let's try to look at sex through our husbands' eyes.

And even beyond that, we need to look at sex from *God's* perspective. Instead of demanding our own way, saying, "I deserve to be loved the way I want to be loved," realize that sex is a gift. One that we sinful humans don't deserve to receive from a holy God.

At this point we could ask, "Who's going to look out for me if *I* don't? I don't want to lose my identity by constantly serving someone else. I am my own person, after all."

Well, Paul seems to think that we can't truly come into our own until we die to ourselves and find our identity somewhere else—namely in Christ. Galatians 2 makes this crystal-clear.

It's inexplicable, but who we are becomes even more individual, real, and beautiful when we deny our own desires and serve others. The world has it backward—putting someone else's needs before your own means you're *strong,* not weak.

We can't do this on our own, however. As Paul says in Romans 7, "I have the desire to do what is good, but I cannot carry it out." You'll hear me chanting this refrain throughout the pages of this book. We desperately need God's help.

Surrender to Him and let His Spirit work in your heart. Ask Him to give you the strength, energy, determination, and desire to begin meeting your husband's physical needs more often and more willingly.

Sometimes our feelings will get hurt, and our sex drive will shut down. We won't want sex until everything is right. When things aren't perfect, though, we desperately need God yet again. He promises He'll be there to help us.

If you're anything like me, there have been plenty of times when you prayed halfheartedly for something, not believing that God would actually come through for you or even bother listening to your prayer.

We're told in James chapter 1 that we will face trials. But if we ask in faith—if we believe and not doubt—God will give us wisdom generously. (I'm sure the trials James speaks of include those of marriage.) But when we ask for something and don't really believe God can accomplish it, we're like "a wave of the sea, blown and tossed by the wind."

Praying for a renewed sexual relationship with your husband will always be in line with God's wisdom and His perfect will for your life. And when you pray in complete faith, He promises to answer, as Jesus indicates in Matthew 21.

Ask your God for a complete sexual relationship makeover. He will give you sexual desire even when it seems like an impossible request. But you have to ask. And believe with all your heart—even if you can't see or understand how it will all play out—that the results will be amazing.

Chapter 2

Male and Female He Created Them

The facts are the facts: Men and women are different. Our Creator designed us that way.

The problem lies in our negative perception of that fact. The idea that different equals bad. The belief that if my husband were more like *me*, life would be better.

We've got to realize, though, that God made men and women different, separate, distinct *before* the fall, so it must have been a part of Plan A—His original, holy, sin-free, perfect Plan.

Contrary to what seems to underlie a lot of popular opinion, God did not make Adam and Eve the same, only to have Adam take a bite of the apple and instantly become less like Eve and more like the "typical male" today. Sure, I've thought it, too—"In a perfect world, my husband would be more like *me*—sensitive, romantic, thoughtful, in tune with his emotions (and mine, too)."

Not so. Yes, there was plenty of fallout from the Fall. And no, we don't know a whole lot about Adam before he took The Bite. But we have no evidence to support our notion that men were a lot more like women before all that happened.

Did men and women get along better? Sure! After all, it's not like they had money troubles or sexual dysfunction—or in-laws, for crying out loud! But were men and women inherently more alike than they are now? I don't think so. Therefore, our differences are not the issue. How we *deal* with them is.

God didn't create us with a humongous libido gap, knowing full well we'd go crazy trying to bridge it. I do believe there's a gap, but a big chunk of it is society-driven:

- Men are bombarded with sexual images day in and day out, which serves to fuel (at a furious pace) the sex drive they've already got.
- Women are bombarded with negative messages about men, which takes their emotionally driven sex drive down a notch or two (or six).

Not what God had in mind.

"Instead of reflecting true, God-instituted variances," Dr. Tim Alan Gardner says in *Sacred Sex,* "much of the Mars and Venus drivel is simply an excuse to justify certain selfish behaviors. God calls us to serve one another, not to rationalize or whine."

God's original design included distinct differences between men and women, but it did *not* include all the controversy, contempt, and cat-fighting we have today. All that junk is a direct product of the Fall.

How Are We Different?

We know the basic external physical differences between men and women. You've got the facial/chest hair thing, the private parts thing, and the body build thing, and that's about it, give or take a few other minor details.

No one is arguing over the differences in physical makeup, but only recently have scientists and psychologists started admitting what Christians have known all along—men and women are different on the *inside* as well. We're not just different because we've been raised differently. We were *born* different.

Give a little girl a small plank of wood, and chances are she'll cradle it like a baby or use it as a prop in a romantic drama. Give a little boy the same plank, and it becomes a rifle or a grenade. Or a baseball bat or bludgeon.

We women are lovers and nurturers. Our men are protectors and providers.

Men and women were also created with different hormones present in different levels. I read recently about a strange phenomenon—a testosterone bath of sorts that a male child experiences while still in the womb. It serves to give him more masculine traits and also severs some of the nerve endings that connect the brain's right and left hemispheres. No, it doesn't kill his brain cells. (I know what you're thinking.) It just separates his thoughts into different parts.

What this essentially means is that women are better able to juggle many things at once, while men tend to be better at focusing on a single thing. Unfortunately for us, this also means we're more easily distracted—during sex in particular. (More on this in chapter 7.)

Women are like those impossibly complicated controlboards in a sound booth, with a million possible combinations of off/on/anywhere-in-between. Men are more like a light switch. Flip it on, and that's it.

The difference in hormone levels also influences our sex drives significantly. A guy's testosterone levels are pretty much constant, while a woman's hormones vary greatly with her menstrual cycle. Some days I feel like writing a poem for my husband—"My Love Is Like an Ocean." How's this for an opener?

> *Darling, please know*
> *my hormones ebb and flow.*
> *When the tide is low,*
> *the answer's NO!*

Okay, maybe I'll stick to prose.

What other differences are there? Well, there's the whole concept of sexual pressure building up in a man's body, with a definite need to release it. I don't think it's quite a matter of a man needing sex at least once a week or he'll die. But their bodies *are* way different than ours, and if a man's body says he needs to release this pent-up tension, he'll have a hard time keeping a lid on it. It's not that women can't crave sex, but we're lacking that built-in pressure cooker. Our desire can diminish without sexual release.

Why did God make us differently? For lots of reasons—some I understand, some I don't. For one, so we'll be attracted to and fascinated by each other. There's something mysterious—and fabulous—about the bond that is created between two people who are so different, yet become one.

We're different so we'll complement each other, balance each other, be strong where the other is weak. We're different so we'll have to work at developing an intimate relationship.

In fact, both men and women inherited their best traits from their Maker Himself. Men are strong and courageous. Women—tender and sensitive. How amazing that we can be so different yet both reflect the character of God.

Playing on the Same Turf

Men and women are also different when it comes to communication. And we women often expect our husbands to be the ones who bridge this aspect of the gender gap. After all, isn't it *his* job to open up, share his emotions, and get in touch with his "feminine side"? When it comes to talking, women *are* the superior gender, right?

I have an idea, girls. I'm thinking of something crazy—off the wall. What if, just for once, *we* decided to be the ones to move to the middle—and beyond? What if we took the time to learn how our husbands best give and receive information and work with that?

On average, women talk way more than men. Men typically use words out of necessity. We talk just for fun. What if we (gasp!) cut down on the amount of words we use when speaking to our husbands?

It's actually biblical to talk less than most of us do. "When words are many," one of the proverbs says, "sin is not absent, but he who holds his tongue is wise."*

What if we decided to talk more sparingly, to chop down what we

---

* Proverbs 10:19.

have to say, to edit it, to make it more palatable to our husbands? What if we filtered our words through a checklist of sorts? "Will this information benefit my husband?" "Can I say this in a way that will grab his attention?" "Can I say what needs said before his eyes glaze over?"

Timing is also important when communicating with your husband. Women are adept at talking and doing three other things all at once. Men like to focus on one thing at a time. I've learned this the hard way. When Gabe is at his computer, in the middle of a big project, it's not wise to launch into the details of something that isn't urgent.

Another tip—don't put him on the spot. Men often need time to think things over before they give you an answer. We women work out our troubles by talking through them. Men tend to *think* on things without verbalizing, and *then* they talk. Not a bad habit for us women to adopt— thinking before we speak.

Take your husband at his word. Guys usually say what they mean. Don't overanalyze what you think might be hidden meanings behind their words. Men see things in black and white. Say what you mean. Say it succinctly. Don't beat around the bush. Forget the subtle hints. Scrap the mind games. He doesn't have a crystal ball.

You take the steps to better communication. *You* move toward that elusive middle ground. Show him that you're willing to play on *his* turf.

Just the Facts, Ma'am

I'm not suggesting you give your husband the silent treatment. Just don't bombard him with millions of details and stories every evening. He's sure to be more genuinely interested in the three or four select items of business you share. To borrow a concept from SportsCenter, a guy favorite, what if we condensed our day into a two-minute highlight clip in lieu of an entire six-hour doubleheader?

Try talking less about you and asking him about his day instead. This is especially good advice for stay-at-home moms. Yes, your day was rough and you spent it with toddlers and had no intellectual stimulation. But he's important too. Have another outlet available for your tales of the day. Call a girlfriend. Keep a journal. Post a blog.

Husbands can sense when you're doing this, and they will appreciate you for it.

Inside a Man's Heart

If women like to express themselves to their husbands using *words,* what expression do men prefer? Hmmm…how about sex?

In order to experience true oneness with our mates, we need both parts, and God knew that. He could have equipped both sexes equally in both areas, letting us take what might seem to be the easy route, but He didn't. Generally speaking, men got the physical; we got the verbal. When we learn to speak our lover's language and not just our own, we're on our way to true intimacy.

Just because men can't always put into words how sex affects them emotionally doesn't mean it doesn't. Sex with his wife can be deeply, intensely emotional for a guy. Your husband feels a oneness with you during sex that is unparalleled.

Yes, men should try to express their true feelings to us verbally, but on our side, we should be more open to meeting our husbands' sexual needs, realizing this makes them feel closer to us emotionally.

It's give and take. We women give to a lot of people, but when it comes to our husbands, we often just take. And harp and complain when we think they're not giving enough. "He's just using me for sex," we whine self-righteously. And what are we using *him* for? A wedding ring? His sperm? His strong arms? His earning power? When we make ignorant and hurtful comments about men thinking of nothing but sex, we're not being fair.

Sex is not equal to men and women. It's not fair to judge our husbands according to our framework. They weren't built the same. His desire for sex is no more wrong or out of proportion than my desire for emotional connection and affection. After all, are we willing to look at spending time with us as something our husbands should only have to do when they "feel like it"?

We want our husbands to share their emotions with us, but then we often dictate the method. We insist they verbalize what they feel rather than express it physically through sex.

Physical needs are the ones we women shove to the side when other, more "valid" needs are pressing. We get by on little sleep, fill our bodies with sugar and caffeine, and neglect exercise. Emotional needs are more important, right?

But for a guy, sex *is* emotional. It meets emotional needs deep within his soul.

He's Not Asking for Much. Really.

It feels good to feel feminine and sexy. And it's very important to your husband that he feel like a man. His masculinity is wrapped up in a handful of basic things, including his ability to provide for his family and his sexual prowess.

Sex, to your husband, isn't all about him. It's about *you*. How you respond to him is a huge part of his identity. He wants to be your hero. He'd give anything to be able to make you go crazy in bed.

When asked, men acknowledge they are just as thrilled—if not more so—watching their wives reach orgasm as they are having one themselves. We women are often more interested in *receiving* pleasure than *giving* it. Seems to me that when it comes to sex, men are a lot more unselfish than women.

I love what Celia told me about her husband. "After a romp in the sheets that was so rowdy my throat hurts afterward, he's got a grin on his face that lasts for a week!"

When you want him, *need* him sexually, that gives him purpose and motivation in all areas of his life. When he feels rejected sexually, the opposite is true. He feels destroyed.

When your husband communicates his desire to make love to you, he is making himself incredibly vulnerable. He's risking emotional rejection, which is ultimately a slam on his manhood.

We women aren't dumb. We pick up on our husband's vulnerability, and we know this gives us a huge measure of control. If we want to hurt our husbands or "just put them in their place," withholding our bodies and saying no to sex will do the trick.

Men generally don't ask for a whole lot, though. They're not high-maintenance like us women. Really, they're simple rather than complex—and I mean that in the kindest sense of the word. Simplicity can be refreshing when you've been a complex woman all your life. I hung out with "the guys" a lot while I was in college for that very reason—I needed a break from my species.

Your husband doesn't expect you to be superwoman, just *his* woman. If the sex you share is frequent and exciting and you're a willing participant, your husband isn't going to mind the laundry pile or unvacuumed floor so much. A sexually satisfied man becomes a bit blinded to the petty cares of the world around him. More than that, when you admire and respond to your husband, he feels like he wants to *conquer* the world for you. (Do you want to be queen of the world? You can be!)

Whether or not sex is an actual "need" for a guy is beside the point. It sure *feels* like a need to him, and when we willingly meet that need for our husbands, they become very grateful indeed.

One of the proverbs says that "a longing fulfilled is sweet to the soul." If I say I love my husband and I mean it, why wouldn't I want to do something I know he would love—and that would make him feel loved? Why wouldn't I be happy to fulfill one of his greatest longings and be sweetness to his soul?

"Consider the fact that your husband is not a clueless jerk," Lorilee Craker advises, "so much as he is a guy, subject to random fits of desire for you that may not always fit conveniently into your schedule."

When we gripe and complain about our husbands perpetually wanting sex, we're ignoring an important fact: God made them that way. As the prophet Isaiah writes, Who am I (clay) to argue with God (the Potter) about His creation? God wants your husband to be physically drawn to you—like a magnet—consistently wanting to be close to you.

"I belong to my lover, and his desire is for me," we read in the Song of Songs. Solomon's wife isn't saying this with a roll of her eyes. She is thrilled that her husband wants her. We should be, too.

And goodness gracious, why aren't we honored and flattered when our husbands want us? Why are we put out and annoyed? Don't I want to be wanted? Do I want him to want *someone else* instead? I think not.

Stand Up for Your Man

In her book *Honey, I Don't Have a Headache Tonight,* Sheila Wray Gregoire explores our culture's attack on gender in an eye-opening chapter entitled "Who Wears the Pants in This Family?" In days gone by, people knew what it was to be a man or a woman. In general, each gender respected the uniqueness of the other. Today, men are being stripped of their God-given masculinity and encouraged to get in touch with their "feminine sides."

We've turned our men into whimpering wimps and then we despise them for being wusses with no backbone. "Honey, could you become more like a woman without losing your manhood?" How does *that* work?

Sheila points out that when Susan B. Anthony first began pushing for women's rights, she backed up her position with the Bible. She embraced a woman's God-given roles as wife and mother rather than rejecting them.

Then in the 1960s, a new kind of feminist emerged—anti-male, anti-Bible, anti-gender, anti-marriage. "The feminist movement was no longer a fight for justice and human dignity," Sheila comments, "but instead it became a fight between the sexes, where one side must lose."

Our culture tells us it is perfectly acceptable for us women to bash men for being who God made them—men. Like the bumper stickers that read, "Women who want to be equal to men lack ambition."

In his first letter, the apostle Peter admonishes us to "treat everyone you meet with dignity," as *The Message* puts it. I can't imagine that this excludes half of the human population. And we're sadly mistaken if we think that denigrating men while trying to elevate ourselves will bring us a lick of happiness. It won't.

God never intended for there to be a battle of the sexes. He absolutely created us to be different, but His intent was that we would complement and complete each other—not claw and clash as bitter antagonists.

As women, then, we should celebrate and enjoy our femininity while supporting and encouraging our husbands' masculinity.

Let's make a quick recap of what's important. Sexual intimacy is not inferior to emotional intimacy, no matter what we may think! God doesn't command our husbands to cuddle on the couch with us or bring us roses. He does command us to have sex with our husbands.

Remember—a relationship with someone who is exactly like you in every way doesn't do much for you in the way of developing character. You don't have to be unselfish or sacrificial. You like the same things. You communicate the same way. You understand each other. Not much effort involved. No dying to self.

If that's what you want, don't get married. Get a cat.

We expect our men to do plenty of things they find uncomfortable—share deep feelings, be romantic, buy flowers. Yet we balk at doing anything for them that might take us an inch outside our comfort zones.

It's time to make a change, girls! As followers of Christ, we need to be willing to stand up for our husbands, even if our girlfriends are cracking jokes about their men's sex drives.

No, it's not easy to meet our husband's needs, because their needs are different from ours. But that is our responsibility. And it ultimately leads to our greatest joy.

Chapter 3

And the Bible Says... Get It On!

Which do you think is the more noble pursuit—becoming more *spiritual* or more *sexual*? No-brainer—or trick question?

It's no secret that we typically see *sexual* and *spiritual* as contradictory terms, or at the least, very distantly related. Some of us even look at them as bitter adversaries rather than bosom buddies.

In their book *Intimate Issues,* Linda Dillow and Lorraine Pintus comment on the fact that most Christian women do not include words like *sexual* or *sensuous* in their definitions of a godly woman. "Godly" women love God, help others, read their Bibles, pray for their families, show mercy and hospitality, and do all sorts of other "spiritual" things. We equate physical with worldly and spiritual with godly.

There's just one small problem with all of this. In the process of becoming "godly," we've ignored a huge part of who we are as women—who God created us to be. We are physical beings—*sexual* and *sensual* beings. He could have created us to be angels—spirits without physical forms. He went the physical route for a reason. There are physical things He wanted us to experience, but within the framework of the institution we call marriage, of course.

"When God created us female...He meant for the spiritual and sexual to melt together," the *Issues* sisters say. I agree with the bold assertion that married Christian women should be the greatest lovers on earth. Not only has God given us physical passion, but we possess an additional element that most of the world lacks—holiness.

So why the huge discrepancy between what should be and what is? If we should be the best lovers in the world, why *aren't* we? Linda and Lorraine are blunt:

> For many women, the problem is...their attitude. They
> don't want to "do it" because they have not made a commit-
> ment to God to be the lover He has asked them to be.

It hurts to admit, but not wanting sex is often a *spiritual* problem. If you're consistently denying your husband, you're denying that God has given you an incredibly special gift to personally enjoy and to share with another—and has specifically asked you to use it often. When you say no, you're telling God His gift is inferior. You're throwing it back at Him and saying, "Thanks, but no thanks."

No matter how godly a woman you consider yourself to be, if you haven't surrendered your sex life to God, you might as well throw the word "godly" out the window. We can't pick and choose the parts of our lives we want to give to the Lord. He wants all of us. If you aren't honoring Him in your marriage bed, you aren't honoring Him.

Sex from Hell

We'll look specifically at what God has to say about sex in just a bit, but let's play devil's advocate, so to speak, for a moment. Ever thought about what *Satan* might think about happily married sex?

"Why would Satan think about sex?" you want to know.

I'll tell you why. Our goal as Christians is to love what God, loves and to hate what God hates. As the father of lies (compared to God, who is Truth Himself), Satan hates what God loves and loves what God hates. Since God is a huge proponent of married people having sex, I think it's safe to say that Satan's not a big fan.

Even more, because sexual intimacy between a husband and wife is a picture of Christ's relationship with His church (see Ephesians chapter 5), then I can't think of a better place for Satan to attack us.

You wanna eavesdrop with me on the big bad devil during his weekly pep talk with his little demonly cohorts? Shh...hell's head honcho is starting his speech...

"Okay, crew, here's the plan. We can't do everything, unfortunately, so we're going to have to pick and choose our battles. I have an idea—and it's brilliant.

"Let's make these Christian women *think* they're on the right track 'spiritually.' Let them read their Bibles and go to church and 'reach out' to their neighbors— even witness to someone at work every now and again.

"I want them attacked—are you ready for this?—in the *bedroom.* Make them 'too busy' for sex. Too tired. Too overwhelmed with life. Make them more focused on themselves than on their husbands.

"Plant these thoughts in their pretty little heads: 'It's all about me. If I don't want sex, I shouldn't have to have it. I have my rights. Sex is overrated anyway. Whatever happened to connecting emotionally and spiritually? And besides, my husband has some shaping up to do before he deserves to get lucky.'

"Get creative in your thought-planting. Even outrageous. They'll believe anything, especially if they hear it from their Christian friends, or better yet, a Bible-study leader.

"Just remember, the key is to make them think that sex is optional—like going out to dinner. It's their prerogative...or not. Something they do when the mood strikes and complain about every other time.

"Whatever you do, keep them from figuring out that their sour attitudes toward sex are sinful and reflect a disobedient heart. Make them think they can be fully surrendered to *Him*—'sold out for Christ,' they like to call it—without handing over the keys to that part of their lives. And do *not,* I repeat, do *not* let them see how spiritual sex really is.

"Feel free to use any and all resources at your disposal. I've got some great magazines and TV shows out this week that will be perfect. A little twist here. A little tweak there. Make them think of sex as nothing more than secular, banal, crude, immoral, and evil.

"Cloud their vision. Close their minds to the truth. Encourage that selfish attitude that keeps welling up inside them.

"C'mon, boys! We've got a job to do! And it's gonna be *fun!*"

Satan's not the only compulsive liar out there. The media is constantly feeding us deceptions about sex. We'd do well to remember one important thing: The Bible came first. It was written long before *Cosmopolitan* or your favorite sitcom. God didn't get *His* ideas about sex from the media. He didn't take something bad and make it good. *He created it good.* His fallen creatures have since corrupted it and gotten it into its current pathetic state.

So do yourself a favor. As you read through some of the things God has to say about sex, think about them with an uncluttered mind. Don't filter God's words through a brain clogged up with what you already know and believe about sex from nonbiblical sources. If we associate sex with evil, we're allowing our culture's abuse of sex to color our thinking.

Because God created sex, what He says about it goes. What anyone else says about it either follows God's original prescription—or it twists His marvelous and brilliant idea into something completely different and wrong.

...And It Was Very Good

Let's start at square one. God makes Adam out of dust. He creates him not as just a spiritual being but as a physical specimen complete with the same special appendages we find on our husbands' bodies today.

When it came time to make a woman—and God created her out of a need he saw expressed in man—He employed a slightly different tactic. He took one of Adam's ribs when he was sleeping, and good ol' Adam woke to find a woman by his side, complete with all the curves and crevices unique to the female species.

We don't know anything about Adam and Eve's first—or subsequent—sexual encounters. We don't know what their bodies looked like either. It's a mystery whether or not Adam was well-endowed or if Eve's cup size was A, B, C, or beyond. I'm sure God purposely chose not to tell us, knowing full well we'd just compare ourselves to them, as we're infamous for doing.

He commanded the couple to be fruitful and multiply and fill the earth. And while they disregarded or disobeyed plenty of God's other commands in their day, they sure heeded and obeyed that one.

We don't know if God personally taught Adam and Eve how to come together in sexual union or if He just sat back and smiled while they figured it out on their own. Whatever the case, sex was good, because God declared that *everything* He made was good. In fact, right after He created the first couple "male and female," He said it was "*very* good."

I can just hear Eve and Adam as they walked through the garden with God one beautiful evening. "Gee, God," Eve says, "about that 'be fruitful and multiply' thing. Thanks a heap for retiring the dust-and-ribs method in favor of this sex stuff. It's awesome! You didn't have to do that!"

Adam, who gets turned on just thinking about it, turns to God and says, "Uh, God, I hate to cut tonight's visit short, but would you mind too terribly much if Evie and I headed back to our fig leaf nest? I just remembered some business we need to take care of."

As if God doesn't know what he's up to.

The Mysterious Analogy

The Bible tells us that oneness with our mate mirrors Christ's oneness with believers, His church. "No one abuses his own body, does he?" Paul asks in Ephesians 5.

> No, he feeds and pampers it. That's how Christ treats us, the church, since we are part of his body. And this is why a man leaves father and mother and cherishes his wife. No longer two, they become "one flesh." This is a huge mystery, and I don't pretend to understand it all. What is clearest to me is the way Christ treats the church.

Sex is as physically close as you can get to another human being (cannibalism aside). Body parts are not only touching—flesh pressed against flesh—but are actually nestled *inside* each other. Wow.

Christ wants intimacy like that with us—as close to Him as we can possibly get, presenting ourselves to Him emotionally open, naked, and unashamed. Intimacy where everything we have and everything we are is offered to Him without reserve, and where we let Him know us and we know Him familiarly and completely.

Paul longed to know Christ like that. "I consider everything a loss compared to the surpassing greatness of knowing Christ Jesus my Lord, for whose sake I have lost all things."*

This analogy—comparing knowing Christ to knowing our mate sexually—can be uncomfortable for us because of our inhibitions and preconceived notions concerning sex. However, those inhibitions are Fall-related, not God-created. The book of Genesis tells us of the first couple, "The man and his wife were both naked, and they felt no shame." Before man sinned, there was no shame in sex, no shame in nakedness, no such thing as shame at all.

The Christian Plain Brown Wrapper

I remember browsing through our church's tiny library as a youngster in the mid '80s. On the tip-top shelf sat a book whose title escapes me at the moment, but I know one of the words in the title was "sex."

I couldn't even reach the shelf with the stool the librarian kept handy, but I was dying to look at the card in the back. I wanted to see who in the church had dared to check out such a scandalous book.

Intended for Pleasure, one of the first Christian books on sex, came out in the 1970s. It was wrapped in cellophane and stocked on bookstores' top shelves like it was an issue of Playboy.

Sex is private (between a man and wife only), and sex is exclusive (between a man and wife only), but sex is not shameful. It is beautiful and holy. The sexual interaction between a husband and wife symbolizes Christ's relationship with us, the ones He loves, so it can't be anything but good.

Rejoice, Revel... and Read On

We know sex is okay for reproduction, and we know it's good because of what it represents, but how much fun are we allowed to have during the act? And more importantly, how crazy should we let it get?

Good news for you, my frisky friend! Though Scripture certainly speaks about species multiplication and representative oneness, it has more to say about the sensual pleasures of sex than all the other stuff combined!

---

* Philippians 3:7.

Enter the Song of Solomon, the Bible's raciest book. "Do you think that God would allow men and women to marry," asks writer and speaker Tommy Nelson, "and then toss them a grenade called intimacy and say to them, 'Well, just fiddle around a little with this and you'll figure out how to work it'? No, indeed not."*

Indeed not. He gave us a wonderful instruction manual—the Song of Songs—nestled right inside the Great Instruction Manual itself.

Frankly, God has made the whole thing pretty clear. He created us with all our female parts, parts that fit perfectly with the parts He gave our husbands. He designed us with five distinct senses He expects us to use. He made us with the ability to give and receive sexual pleasure with our husbands. He gave us the Song of Songs that intimately examines the sexual delights available to a man and his wife. He wants us to experience and enjoy His creation, especially His creation of sex.

There is no biblical basis for holding back, for guarding yourself or your emotions when it comes to sex with your husband. It's God's desire that we rejoice and revel in the sensations and pleasures and passions He has given us as a precious gift.

May you "rejoice in the wife of your youth," says the book of Proverbs. "May her breasts satisfy you always, may you ever be captivated by her love."

Unbelievers are using God's gift every day, but because they don't recognize it as such, they often abuse it or don't appreciate it in its fullness.

Are you an obedient child of God? Are you consistently obeying all of your Father's commands? Even the one that says you should be having sex with your husband on a regular basis?

When we're enjoying sex, we're pleasing our Creator. God wants you and your husband to have sex! Good, good sex—and lots of it! Unbelievable, isn't it? I can see it now. Your face is turning pink, and you're wondering why you even started reading this book in the first place. Keep reading, my friend! We've only just begun!

---

* I really didn't understand this book until I attended Tommy Nelson's Song of Solomon conference a couple years ago. A lot of great stuff has been written about this book of the Bible, especially in the last few years, so instead of borrowing everyone else's commentaries and ideas, I'll let you check out a couple books on your own. *The Book of Romance* by Tommy Nelson and *Intimate Issues* by Linda Dillow and Lorraine Pintus are great resources to help you understand this passion-packed little book more completely.

ROADBLOCKS TO GREAT SEX

Chapter 4

Ghosts from the Past

We live in a day and age of sexual "freedom," where having sex with whomever, whenever is your prerogative. No strings attached. No questions asked.

At least that's the picture Hollywood paints.

Deep down inside, we all know it's a big fat lie. Sex outside of marriage has serious consequences to every part of our being. And Christian or no, many of us women are faced with the effects of our past sexual choices on a daily basis.

I was a virgin when I met my husband, squeaky clean by the world's standards. But it wasn't any fun telling Gabe about a past relationship that I know crossed *God's* boundaries. Gratefully, Gabe forgave me, and the matter was forever dropped.

Sure, there are women who did much more than "mess around." Women who had sex, more than one time, with more than one man. That twisted, balled-up knot of pain and shame in their guts must be excruciating at times. You may be one of them.

But I know God can forgive. I asked for forgiveness, and I am clean.

"Forget the former things," God tells us in Isaiah. "Do not dwell on the past."

Wallowing in our guilt just gives Satan the edge he's been searching for. It's like telling him, "You've successfully robbed me of one of God's greatest gifts—the enjoyment of sex." Not only that, but it says to God, "Your Son's sacrifice wasn't enough to take away this sin of mine."

It can also be a cop-out when it comes to our marriages. "Sex can never be as good as it's supposed to be since I messed up so badly. I might as well not even try."

Another point for Satan.

You *can* move past your past, and you *must* move past your past. You can't do it alone, but you can do it. You owe it to yourself, your husband, and your Savior.

Effects from the Past

I surveyed a large number of women for this book. Nearly half of them (and they were almost all Christians) said they had sex or fooled around with someone other than their husband before they were married.

What effect did their past have on the present?

> "I never had sex, but I fooled around. Sometimes my husband thinks I'm not interested in being romantic because I'm not attracted to him or because I 'used it all up.'"

> "I sometimes recall these episodes and feel terrible about myself and again ask God for forgiveness."

> "It made me not like sex very much—I felt like I was just used for sex."

> "There was heavy petting and oral sex in one relationship and minor indiscretions in a couple others. The former left me with unfair expectations for sex."

> "I had one other partner, and I was really in love with him. Having sex before I married my husband ruined several aspects of sex for me."

> "Biggest mistake of my life. The regret, memories, and comparisons haunt me every day. And the lack of self-control permeated all facets of my life."

How Much to Share

There's really no perfect answer to the question, "How much of my past should I share with my spouse?"

Some experts might say, "None." Others might say, "Everything." My advice would be to pray for wisdom before saying anything.

On the one hand, you don't want to keep deep, dark secrets from your spouse. But you don't want to give every single detail either. You want to spare him from hurtful visual images that could haunt him every time you make love.

You want your husband to be able to trust you, and part of that is being truthful about your past. But as Dr. Kevin Leman says, "It is a gift to your spouse to let some memories die in the past and remain only with you." For a husband and wife to be truly intimate, they must learn to forgive and forget sexual misconduct in each other's past. This is much easier to do if you don't know all the dirty details.

For example, Jenny will have an easier time forgetting that her husband "lost his virginity in college to a former girlfriend" than forgetting that he "dated a voluptuous blonde named Cindy, who seduced him in her dorm room by slowly undressing, putting her naked breasts in his face, leading him to the bed…"

Do you get what I'm saying? Being honest can consist in acknowledging a wrong and asking for forgiveness—without sharing sordid, hurtful details just to get them off your chest.

Holly's Story

I have a wonderful friend, Holly (not her actual name), who I greatly respect and admire. If I look half as great as she does when *I'm* nearing 40, I'll be singing hallelujah! She's fit, trim, and gorgeous, with a brilliant smile that's as genuine as they come. She's outgoing and friendly, and a true woman of God. She's even got a gorgeous husband and kids and lives in a beautiful home.

Sounds perfect, doesn't she? Well, she's not. Holly's got a sexual past that can still haunt her if she doesn't carefully guard her God-forgiven heart.

When I first sent out my surveys for this book, I asked that the recipients keep themselves anonymous. But Holly felt compelled to let me know who she was. "I am so proud of you, Marla," she wrote, "and I want to help you write a book that helps other women in this sensitive area. Call me if you need to!"

I took her up on her offer and was more than blessed by the words of wisdom she had to share. I think you will be too. Feel free to "listen in" on our interview.

Holly, what kinds of thoughts enter your mind when you're reminded of your sexual past?

"Plaguing regret and shame. Regret is a common thread in my life because the sin of fornication was only a symptom of my sad, early life of not loving and cherishing Jesus Christ as my only true love.

"I'm learning that regret is a tool of Satan's that I must stomp on and replace with thankfulness to Jesus for all the grace and mercy He shows me moment by moment. Shame is prevalent when I see or think of the men I have been with. I wonder how much to share with my kids so they'll learn from me. It all stinks. If only I had said NO."

What do you do when you're faced with feelings of guilt and regret?

"I pray a bunch. I cry out to my heavenly Father, and He reassures me of His constant, unconditional, unwavering love. I look at all of the blessings I have despite my sinful past and am reminded it is by grace I am saved and will stay saved. And I ask God how I can use my ashes (sin) for His and others' beauty. Like contributing to this book!"

What helpful tips do you have for a young married woman who is really struggling with her past?

"Remember and read about the promise of forgiveness in His Word. Your sin is no worse than anyone else's—and don't let anyone tell you it is. Fall in love with Jesus and your husband. Pray to forget your sexual past. And flourish in your God-given, God-ordained sexual present. That is what grace and mercy are all about. The Lord wants you to have a vibrant and fulfilling sex life with your husband. Pray for it! Ask and you will receive. And teach others from your mistakes!"

Anything else you'd like to add?

"This is a great service you are doing, Marla. You are taking my ashes and turning them into beauty for God's glory. Bless you, babe!"

The Old and the New

To get over a sexual past, you've got to let go of the old and cling to the new. These words from Colossians 2 tell us what happens to our "old" when we come to Him:

> When you were dead in your sins...God made you alive with Christ. He forgave us all our sins, having canceled the written code...he took it away, nailing it to the cross.

Once you accept Christ as your Savior, His death cancels out every sin you've ever committed and every sin you'll ever commit. Tough to believe, but it comes straight from the Word of God.

Sometimes we might try to "do penance" for our sins by remembering and rehashing them in our minds. This is just a Satan-tool to keep us from feeling God's love and forgiveness. Anytime we're focusing on our past sins, there's no room for dwelling on God's love. It diminishes Christ's sacrifice on the cross that obliterated those very sins.

So what is the "new" we're to embrace? God's principles, His thoughts, the truth of His Word. Verses that remind us that we are clean, whole, righteous, and holy.

"He has reconciled you by Christ's physical body through death to present you holy in his sight, without blemish and free from accusation," Paul tells us in Colossians 1.

"Fortunate those whose crimes are carted off," is the way *The Message* paraphrases Romans 4, "whose sins are wiped clean from the slate. Fortunate the person against whom the Lord does not keep score."

Dealing with Flashbacks

We can try our hardest to repress the past, to forget things ever happened, but memories often come popping up when we least expect them—and at the worst possible moments.

Flashbacks can be a painful obstacle to overcome on your way to a flourishing sexual relationship with your mate. Because sex is such an emotional experience, flashbacks bring with them not only a recall of physical details, but feelings and emotions as well.

Even though God completely forgives us, He doesn't promise that we will never have to deal with repercussions of a sinful past. As Dr. Leman points out in his book *Sheet Music,* "While God removes the stain, he doesn't always remove the consequences." He suggests that if you have flashbacks of former sexual partners, "you'll need to learn on a case-by-case basis, how to turn your attention back to your spouse."

Like it or not, a bond is created between two people when they have sex—whether they're married or not. Ask God to break the ties that bind you to another and strengthen and bless the ties that bind you to your husband. Don't ever choose to replay the flashback tapes in your mind. That will do nothing more than strengthen your bond with a former lover.

The devil tries to use flashbacks to shift your focus from what God has done for you to how you have failed in the past. As a child of God, Satan has no power over you—he has only the power you choose to give him. "Do not give the devil a foothold," we read in Ephesians 4.

"Submit yourselves, then, to God. Resist the devil, and he will flee from you," James encourages us. Command Satan to leave you—throw Scripture verses in his face that declare the truth: He is powerless against you.

"By embracing death, taking it into himself, he [Christ] destroyed the Devil's hold on death and freed all who cower through life," says the writer of Hebrews.

"Finally, be strong in the Lord and in his mighty power. Put on the full armor of God so that you can take your stand against the devil's schemes."*

Commit these verses to memory—or post them somewhere you can see them when you need them most.

Looking for the Good

I don't claim to know all the good God can bring out of a tragic situation like a sexually sinful past. But I can think of at least two things that can be positive results.

First of all, a woman with a sexual history can bring much encouragement to someone in the midst of a similar struggle. When we are

---

* James 4:7; Hebrews 2:14 MSG; Ephesians 6:10-11.

fighting an intense battle against a particular sin, the last thing we need is to be preached at by someone who has never failed in this area.

How comforting to hear another woman (like my sweet friend Holly) share that she committed the same exact sin yet has found forgiveness, healing, and peace in the loving arms of her Savior. We gain strength from someone who has learned that her worth as a person is not measured by her behavior, past or present, but by the unfathomable love God has for her as His child.

God knows everything you've done and still loves you deeply. Wow.

And the second good that can come of a sexual past? Women with a sexual past can often appreciate real, true sexual intimacy with their husbands in a more profound way because they've experienced the negative side of sex. As Tommy Nelson says so well, "It is very often the person who has been on the opposite side of good who knows the most about good."

Who better to write about the beauty of true love and married sexuality in the Song of Songs than Solomon, a guy who blew it big time by having hundreds of wives and concubines? Think of people with wretched pasts that God chose to use in powerful ways—Paul the apostle and the prostitute who wiped Jesus' feet with her hair come to mind. And in the genealogy of Jesus, we see names of women (Bathsheba, Rahab, and Tamar) who committed sexual sins.

God can use your failures to touch the lives of others. And they often make a more powerful statement of His love and grace than the things you did *right* in your life. His strength is made perfect in our weakness.

"Technical Virginity"

Even if your sexual slate was clean *before* your hubby entered the picture, your premarital sexual past with him can also cause much grief and heartache in your life together. God doesn't tell us to abstain from premarital sex "until you find the right one." He says no sex before marriage, period. Engagement rings don't count for squat.

Yes, Gabe and I made it to our wedding night with our technical virginity soundly intact, but I would have been mortified had anyone witnessed one of our after-hours cuddling and kissing sessions while we were engaged.

In my heart, I knew what we were doing was wrong, but I didn't realize until after our wedding that it would also be detrimental to our sex lives as newlyweds. In the beginning, when intercourse hurt and orgasms were hard to come by, I wanted the premarital "good ol' days" back.

I finally understood for myself why God says to wait—all the way. My technical virginity wasn't *real* virginity at all. I had sacrificed something very special and important by choosing to indulge in some late-night feel-good sessions while we were dating. What regret!

Satan had his way with me. He convinced me that giving in "just a little" wasn't "going all the way." I listened to his lies, and I paid for it.

"We didn't have sex, but we did mess around," one newly married woman told me. "He would lie on top of me and kiss me while we were on the couch 'watching' TV. He would touch my rear end and I'd be so aroused that I'd have what I later realized was an orgasm. Now I can't have an orgasm during sex, but if I just get on top of him with my underwear on, he can sometimes give me an orgasm like before."

Another woman said, "I believe it made us feel like we'd crossed a boundary we should have waited for the wedding night to cross. I think it took some of the magic of that first night away."

I know the feeling.

And the Survey Says...

Roughly one-fourth of the women I surveyed did more than "mess around." They had sex with their husbands before they tied the knot. Here's what some of them had to say about it:

> "There was a lot of guilt for a while when we realized we may have missed something more that God had for us."

> "Sometimes it becomes an issue and we argue about it, because when we have those 'dry' spells, or it doesn't

seem quite as good as you think it should be, my husband thinks it's because of that and compares it to previous occasions."

"I feel I'm being punished for this even though I've asked for forgiveness. I can't enjoy sex at all. I hate to even think about it."

"It about ruined our marriage. Every time I would have an orgasm, I would feel a wave of guilt afterward. That created a habit I brought into my marriage."

"It definitely ruined the excitement of being newly-weds. Sometimes I wonder if I can't achieve orgasm because I'm being punished by God."

Several mentioned the negative impact their sexual pasts would have on their kids. "We have regrets that we didn't wait and feel guilty," one woman told me. "It will be difficult to discuss this with our children in the future because we didn't do the right thing."

Another woman who had sex before she was married said, "It will probably have more of an effect when our kids start asking us those questions…ouch."

I feel the same way, and I am not looking forward to that day. Too bad I was only thinking of myself—not our future children (or God or anyone else)—when I gave into temptation before marriage.

Deceptions

One woman who was struggling in her sexual relationship with her husband had an interesting take on their decision to wait until marriage for sex.

"Sometimes I think that because we waited until marriage, sex was a real letdown for both of us," she says. "We expected to do it so much more often than we have. Sometimes I wonder if waiting so long and trying so hard to be good gave us the idea that 'sex is bad,' and now we can't get out of the pattern."

Her point may be valid, but I have another theory.

Part of the problem is our unrealistic view of sex before we've actually experienced it. The media in particular has led us to believe that "normal" men and women are hot and horny a hefty percentage of the time. That is not the case—at least not for women. One of the biggest misconceptions young brides have about marriage is that they will want to have sex at least ten times a week—if not more. That's just not realistic.

Author Sheila Wray Gregoire says she is especially disturbed by magazines and the sensual images of sexy (slutty, really) women on their covers. She says we internalize the messages they send, including the belief that women want sex all the time:

> Before we're married, it's easy to believe it. We have no contrary evidence. When we do marry and find out that our sex drives don't require us to act like rabbits twice a day, we're heartbroken. We wonder what's wrong with us. It's not only our husbands who feel cheated; we do, too.

She says that this wouldn't be nearly so big a problem if society was more honest about sex. "If the women on television weren't as eager to jump into bed as their partners, regardless of what had happened during the day, our husbands might not expect us to act in the same way."

I try to steer clear of sitcoms—and that's why. In the past, I've found myself subconsciously comparing myself/my husband/my sex life with what I've witnessed on a 30-minute television program—a show where actors were getting paid thousands of dollars to pretend that sex was always hot and heavy. The comparisons are hardly fair.

Sheila urges us to realize that the time has come to reclaim what is "normal." And "normal" is not what you see on magazines or on TV. We need to stop comparing ourselves to other people—especially people who aren't even real. What matters most is what makes you and your husband happy and satisfied.

Your television can be a chief enemy of a healthy sex life, concludes Sheila:

> It shows unrealistic relationships, tantalizes with beautiful bodies, and helps *you* feel inadequate and *him*

tempted, all at the same time! Switch off, and both of you are more likely to "turn on" appropriately.

Post-Wedding Blahs

"Why don't I want sex like I did before I was married?" a friend asked me not too long ago. She and her husband had married as virgins.

I told her it could be a number of things but that it often boils down to our insatiable craving for forbidden fruit. The fact that sex is off-limits when you're dating makes it seem all the more tantalizing.

Sex, for women, is more emotional than anything else. Dating is an emotional high, and it stimulates sexual desire. Once you're married, you slowly (or quickly) drift down from that emotional cloud, and your sex drive often comes drifting right down with you.

Before you were married, there was always the element of "someone could catch us any second" or "we shouldn't be doing this." Risk heightens arousal. However, there's little risk involved in making love to your husband…with a wedding band on your finger…in the bedroom you lawfully share.

Another thing that's been missing since your dating days is going days or weeks at a time without seeing your honey pie—allowing the anticipation of your next meeting to build. Most married couples see each other every day, and in some not-so-sexy moments.

There's Hope—And Lots of It

If you waited for sex and you find yourself disappointed in it, keep reading and don't despair. Perhaps you had lovely visions of sex coming naturally, of your desire for your husband being ever-present, of every sexual experience bringing more pleasure than the last. Even if you'd never had sex, you surely had preconceived ideas of how amazing it would be.

We all did. And it *can* be amazing. But it takes time, and it takes work. It does not come easily or naturally. That is a myth. Waiting for marriage helps a lot, but good married sex takes much more than that.

And if you are someone who messed around or had sex before marriage, I hope you no longer feel alone. You aren't suffering by yourself while the rest of the world overcame their past years ago and has moved on to a life of perpetual sexual enjoyment. And hopefully you're beginning to understand some of the reasons why your marriage is struggling in the sex department.

Our past affects us—even if it was just with our husbands-to-be.* But there is hope and forgiveness for all of us. Ask God for that forgiveness today. And then move on to the present and future with the husband He gave you.

Finally, get rid of unrealistic expectations and learn to work with what you've got—real life. And don't think that means you have to settle for less. When it comes to your sexual relationship with your husband, real life can be whatever you choose to make it. And there's lots more about how to do that in the following pages.

---

* Some of you may be suffering from other events in your past, such as sexual abuse, rape, or an abortion. Those devastating things are beyond the realm of what I'm going to deal with in this book. If you need to ask forgiveness, or lack the ability to forgive someone else, I encourage you to seek out someone who can give you the help you need.

Chapter 5

Body Image Blues

I f you were shown a line-up of ten women, ranging in appearance from drop-dead gorgeous to quite homely, who would you say has a better time in bed? The one who most closely resembles a Victoria's Secret model?

As a society, we have come to equate physical perfection with fabulous sex, but I happen to know women at both ends of the spectrum who blow that theory to bits. Among them are a gorgeous woman who battles insecurity and has trouble being sexually responsive to her husband…and an overweight woman with average features who "loves sex" and "orgasms 99 percent of the time."

The truth is, while physical beauty does play a role in sex, it's not as relevant as we seem to think. It's not as relevant as, say, a good attitude, lots of effort, and the quality of your relationship outside the bedroom.

Dr. Tim Gardner shares some enlightening thoughts about the "cultural circus" that defines our perception of "sexy." You've got to be thin with large breasts and "the willingness to reveal absolutely as much skin as allowed by law," he says. No saggy boobs, big hips, fat cells, blemishes, wrinkles, or stretch marks. He concludes, though, as follows:

> If you believe that having bigger breasts, a tighter stomach, or a fuller head of hair will increase your sexual enjoyment, and that your emotional intimacy will skyrocket, you've bought into the "great bodies equal great sex" lie. It's time to hear the truth.

In my heart I know the truth. The beautiful people don't always have the best sex. Got it. Why do I have such a hard time internalizing that fact? Why do I keep believing the lies?

Why am I still bothered by my imperfect teeth, the shape of my nose, the size of my chest, and the toll that childbearing has taken on the remainder of my body parts?

Why do I constantly compare myself to the beauties on TV? Or even the 15-year-olds at church?

Why do I wish I had the money for professional teeth whitening, new highlights every month, and my own personal trainer?

Why do I worry that since I've turned 30, it's all going to be downhill from here?

Why do I fantasize about life with a nice set of boobs?

Eyes at Breast Level

Speaking of boobs, I have a problem. I might as well admit it.

I stare at women's chests.

Just the other day, while spending a day at the pool with my girls, I checked out the top half of every woman who walked by. I can't help it. I might look at a stranger's face for a moment, but then my gaze drifts quickly down to her breasts. Maybe I want to see how much bigger hers are than mine. On the rare occasion that I spot an attractive woman with a chest comparable to mine in size, I smile. I'm going to be okay.

I once asked a friend if she ever stared at other women's breasts.

"Nope. Never."

Okay, it was official. I was weird.

"I stare at their rear ends," she said with a smile.

Say what? And then it hit me. My friend didn't need to stare at women's boobs. She had a perfectly good set of her own. Nice, big, round, firm. What she longed for was a cute little round bottom. Hence the staring farther south.

I liked my rear just fine and wasn't all that concerned about those belonging to other women. Isn't it crazy how obsessed we can become with what we don't have?

Gabe and I were watching a news program the other night, and a certain celebrity was being interviewed for her part in a hurricane relief effort. I didn't hear a word she said; I was mesmerized by her un-Hollywood-like small chest and the fact that she was still sexy. I made a comment to Gabe about the hope this gave me.

"You're looking at her *boobs?*" he asked incredulously.

"I always look at women's boobs," I said. "You know that." We'd discussed it many times before.

"I wish women didn't even *have* boobs," he remarked with a sigh.

I slyly reminded him of his comment the next night in bed. We both laughed, knowing what he had actually meant by his remark—"I wish cup size wasn't such a big deal to women, so you didn't have to worry about yours all the time."

I needed to heed Paul's advice to the Galatians. In chapter 5 of his letter to them, he told them that if they had truly chosen to live a life filled with God's Spirit, they needed to act like it. *The Message* paraphrases it like this:

> That means we will not compare ourselves with each other as if one of us were better and another worse. We have far more interesting things to do with our lives. Each of us is an original.

Must You Increase Your Bust?

Don't worry. I'm not going to ramble on and on about breasts this entire chapter...just a moment longer. Don't want you big-bosomed gals getting bored!

I knew two gals in college who were dissatisfied with their cup size and decided to do something about it. Shortly after they each got married, they traveled many miles together to get boob jobs. Five years later, one of them has long since gotten divorced, and the other's marriage is teetering on the edge of that same fate. Where did the new boobs go wrong?

Dr. Gardner shares the story of Kevin and Brenda, who were struggling with their marriage and sex life and came to him for counseling. Kevin had reached the conclusion that Brenda's breasts were too small for his liking, and feeling self-conscious, she agreed to a breast augmentation.

Her new look increased passion and made Kevin more attentive. Plus, Brenda felt a lot sexier. So far, so good, right?

"Then the law of diminishing returns performed its work," Dr. Gardner continues, "and they were back in my office."

Thankfully, my husband loves and accepts me "as is." It's a priceless comfort. He's opposed to body-part enhancements of all sorts, and even though I fantasize about it periodically, I'm actually relieved.

When I take an honest look at how a boob job might affect my marriage, I can just imagine myself resenting my husband for his fascination with my new and improved bosom.

"Oh, sure—you like me *now!*" I'd scream during a particularly hormonal episode of PMS. "All you care about is your own pleasure!"

Being pregnant for the third time, I've had some insight into this potential scenario. As I write, my boobs are resting peacefully on my blossoming abdomen. In my normal (nonpregnant) state, those two body parts don't even know each other. They live too far apart. In my old age, when my peers will be tucking their breasts into their waistbands, mine probably won't reach that far.

While pregnant, though, I have to be careful not to think resentful thoughts in bed like, "What are *you* so excited about, Mister? You like these better than the *real* me, don't you? You wish I *always* looked like this!"

The problem isn't so much with my body as my attitude. A new chest alone probably wouldn't satisfy me for long. And discontentment with one area of life usually permeates all the others. How is it with you?

Quiz Time

If you could name an improvement to one physical trait of yours, what would it be? Here are some of the answers my survey girls gave: *Thinner thighs. Clearer skin. Smaller rear end. Smoother feet. Less cellulite. Prettier feet. Flatter stomach. Straighter nose. Smaller chest. Bigger chest. Better eyesight. More muscle tone. Smoother legs. Less flab.*

Most of these things can be improved with some hard work and determination, but there's not a whole lot you can do (without surgery) about your not-so-straight nose, your funny-looking feet, or your small boobs.

Before we talk about how body image affects sex with our husbands, let's have fun for just a minute and take a body-image quiz. Answer the following questions as honestly as possible.

1. When you look at your chest in the mirror, your first thought is...
    a. God, why did You do this to me?
    b. Why can't I have boobs at least as big as hers?
    c. Sure, my boobs aren't perfect, but they do the job.
    d. What a rack! I am stacked, baby!

2. What are your honest feelings about your rear end?
    a. I'll never have a nice caboose no matter what I do. Why even try?
    b. If only my rear was cute and round like hers, I'd be happy!
    c. Not bad! My hubby's not complaining!
    d. I stop traffic with this tush!

3. When you look at your legs, what do you see?
    a. Tree trunks. I give up!
    b. My sister-in-law has such loooong legs! How fair is that?
    c. My calves look good, and with a little jogging, I'll bet my thighs could, too.
    d. With legs like these, I should have been a supermodel!

4. What's to like about your hair?
    a. I can't get it to do a single thing! Woe, woe is me!
    b. If only my hair were straight/curly/long/blond like hers!
    c. It's one of my best features.
    d. Everything. I should have been a hair model.

5. Describe your stomach region in five words or less.

   a. Fat, fat, fat, fat, fat.

   b. Never should have had kids.

   c. Sit-ups work wonders.

   d. Washboard. Six-pack. Flat as a pancake. Perfect. Oh, just five words?

6. How often do you obsess or fret over some aspect of your physical appearance?

   a. Once every five minutes.

   b. Every time I see another woman.

   c. About once a week, but then I get over it.

   d. Never. I'm perfect.

7. What is your typical response when your husband compliments a part of your body?

   a. Yeah, right! Whatever! You know I'm ugly and fat!

   b. Too bad I don't look like your old girlfriend!

   c. Thank you, sweetie. You look hot too.

   d. Like I don't already know I'm perfect.

And now for the evaluations. Don't take them too seriously, though—not a one of them is based on any scientific or psychological research whatsoever. Drumroll, please!

- *If you answered mostly a,* you're in the midst of a real struggle with self-pity. You can definitely use some work on your body, but more importantly, you've got to believe you can do it. And that you have been created by God and are well worth the effort!

- *If you answered mostly b,* you're awfully self-conscious and find yourself constantly comparing yourself to others. God made you to be *you,* not anyone else! None of us will ever win the comparison game. There will always be someone out there with bigger this, smaller that, prettier this, and so on. Be the best *you* you can be!

- *If you answered mostly c,* you get the prize! You're doing a great job accepting your body the way it is, but you also realize the importance of hard work to keep it looking good. The older you get, the harder you'll have to work. You can do it, girl!

- I doubt that many of you *answered mostly d,* but if you did, you probably have a hard time keeping friends. Vanity seems to be a glaring problem in your life. Don't forget, sister, that pride cometh before a fall!

Body Image in the Bedroom

Sometimes our struggles with sex can be linked to poor body image. When we don't *feel* sexy, it's hard to *be* sexy. It's easy to get discouraged about our bodies, especially things we can't change.

If I'm of the mind-set that my body is deficient in pleasing my husband in bed, then I'll never be able to make love freely and uninhibitedly.

Beautiful body does not equal sexual pleasure. And conversely, less-than-perfect body does not equal dismal sex life. We need to ask God to clear our minds of the lies of our sick culture so we can accept these facts ourselves. Then we need to pray that He will do the same for our husbands.

I don't know anything about the man you married. Some men, like Brenda's husband, Kevin, are particular about what they like and aren't satisfied unless their wives meet a certain standard. As with Kevin, this may involve deeper issues.

Other men don't get the credit they deserve. They love their wives' bodies, but when they try to tell them that, their women don't believe them for a second.

One thing is true, though—when it comes to our bodies, all husbands don't like the same thing. And their favorite parts aren't always what we might think. I found it quite interesting that many men actually liked body parts that the wives listed as problem areas.

Ladies, can we celebrate the unique and individual bodies God gave each one of us? No matter what parts we have that we're not so fond of, can we make the best of them? Truthfully, your husband may be more helpful in this area than you believe. I think you'll find some reassurance in what I say next.

What Hubby Really Thinks

Aside from those few men who expect physical perfection from their wives, most guys are easily pleased. As long as you make an effort to be attractive and sexy, it really doesn't matter to them that your chest is smaller than average or your thighs are a little bigger than you'd like. (If you find that hard to believe, go back and read "Inside a Man's Heart" in chapter 2 again.)

Don't fall into the "woe is me" trap, where you constantly obsess over yourself and your negative body image. I've realized rather recently how unfair that is to my husband. I whine and complain about my bodily imperfections and don't listen when Gabe says he thinks I'm beautiful and sexy just the way I am. And when I'm stuck on what I lack, I have trouble getting in the mood for sex, and our lovemaking suffers needlessly.

Really, it's not all about you. Forget yourself, act sexy, and maintain a good mood for your hubby's sake. Focus on him, not yourself. And when he says you look good, believe him and accept what he says.

Solomon's lover in the Song of Songs was self-conscious about her appearance—her burnt, ruddy skin in particular—but she didn't let it stop her from making sexual advances to her husband and acting supersensuous.

When it comes to hubbies, it's your attitude that matters most. Dr. Laura puts it this way:

> The vast majority of men feel that attitude, demeanor and behavior take a front seat to perfect skin. When a wife behaves sexily, handles herself alluringly, and by the way she looks at her husband, touches him, and talks to him conveys her interest, love, respect, and attraction, frankly, he'll go anywhere and do anything and slay all dragons for his family.

We all want a dragon-slayer, don't we? And being the hottest little thing around isn't really the key to unlocking the dragon-slayer in your hubby. So what is?

Dressing like a woman. Being sweet-natured. Acting sexy. Flirting with your hubby. Complimenting him. Admiring him. Initiating sex. Not turning him down.

A gorgeous woman who constantly rejects her husband's sexual advances or never has time for him isn't going to look all that beautiful to him for long.

On the other hand, an average, everyday gal who is ready and willing to share sexual pleasures with her husband—and enjoy herself!—will become more and more attractive to him with each passing day.

Accepting Myself

When I'm struggling with accepting my body's quirks and faults, I like to read verses like this one from Psalm 139: "I praise you because I am fearfully and wonderfully made."

It doesn't say I'm perfect, but "wonderful" should be good enough for me.

I'm doing better in the self-acceptance department. I've been telling myself that God gave me imperfect body parts to keep me humble, because He has great things planned for my life. Try it yourself—it's the truth.

There are certain things we can improve about our appearances, and an air of confidence goes a long way too. I've learned that when I'm happy with my body, Gabe is too. But when I whine about something I can change and then don't do anything to change it, it doesn't seem to turn him on.

Speaking of confidence, I also asked women what they *liked* about their bodies. While a few of them couldn't seem to think of a single thing, most of them could list at least one or two parts they were proud of: *Skinny waist. Soft skin. Petiteness. Hair color. Firm breasts. Back. Smile. Thick hair. Thinness and fitness. Toned arms. Feet. Cute toes. Lips. Boobs. Calves. Height. Shape. Hands.*

I may not be able to change everything I don't like, but I do have a measure of control over my appearance.

A healthy, attractive wife is a happier wife. And it will make hubby happier too. I know we've all been handed a different deck of cards to work with—our job is to do the best with what we've got.

Dump the Frump

We each have not-so-great traits we can subtly downplay and beautiful traits we can enhance. Eating right, exercising, new clothes, new makeup, new hairdo—looking good for your husband is never a bad idea.

"Dump the frump, girlfriend," Lorilee Craker exhorts us. "You can do it! I don't care how old you are or how much you weigh. Pretty clothes, underwear and lingerie do come in your size! I truly believe that how we dress deeply influences our sense of self. "

We seem to expect our husbands to woo and romance us, yet we often choose to look frumpy and sloppy. Instead of granny panties and ratty bras, dingy sweats and sloppy ponytails, make an effort to look attractive. You'll feel so much better about yourself! Sexy is as sexy does!

Please don't take this to an extreme, however. I know some women who are so obsessed with their physical appearance that their quest to be attractive takes priority over their husbands.

One husband complained, "My wife says she spends so much time on her body so she can 'look good for her husband,' but she'd rather be at the gym than with me. When she *is* home, she's too busy or tired to share her body with me anyway."

Any time you take to beautify yourself in any way should be carved out of whatever personal time you already have—not hubby time. Most husbands would rather have you hanging on to an extra ten pounds than be too tired or busy for sex.

Our relationship with Christ is also more important than getting in shape. As Paul tells Timothy, "physical training is of some value, but godliness has value for all things, holding promise for both the present life and the life to come."

⌒

Embrace who you are right at this moment—love the person God made you to be. Look at yourself through God's eyes. You're a creature He loves. He created you in His very own image.

God sees the beauty of your spirit. That's what gives you your worth, not your body. Very few of us will ever stack up to society's standard of "beauty," but that's not what matters. "Charm is deceptive, and beauty is fleeting; but a woman who fears the LORD is to be praised," says one of the proverbs.

"What matters is not your outward appearance," Peter tells us, "...but your inner disposition. Cultivate inner beauty, the gentle, gracious kind that God delights in."*

Accepting your body won't happen overnight. Ask God each day to give you positive thoughts about your body—the body He created on purpose for you.

Once you've accepted yourself, start taking small but purposeful steps toward a healthier version of the self you already love. Downplay your problem parts and accentuate the positives. Do your best with what you've been given, and then let it go!

"Beauty does not come from having a perfect body," Sheila Wray Gregoire reminds us. "Beauty truly bubbles up from within, and when we cultivate our characters, allowing ourselves to live a life of abundance, and reveling in the grace that God has given us, we will be beautiful."

---

* 1 Peter 3:3-4 MSG.

Chapter 6

When *He's* Not Interested

This chapter was somewhat of an afterthought. I wasn't convinced it was necessary—until I had an enlightening conversation with a very honest friend.

As a small group of us girls sat around shooting the breeze, the topic of sex came up. The general consensus was that our husbands want it a lot, and we needed to figure out some creative ways to bridge the libido gap.

Then my friend Anne boldly spoke up. "I feel like a freak," she said. She went on to candidly explain that there was definitely a libido gap in her marriage, but that *she* was the one who wanted the sex, not her husband. And when she initiated it, more often than not, she got shot down.

I can't speak from experience, but I can imagine that Anne's situation is emotionally painful on several levels. In our society, men are touted as always wanting sex. When your husband doesn't, what does that say about *you*, you wonder? How do you handle the careless comments of friends who hear your plight and say, "I wish I had *your* problem! My husband is *constantly* asking for sex. Ugh!"

Anne looked to me, "the resident sex expert" (it's amazing what people think you know just because you're writing a book), for some advice. I honestly had no idea what to say, but I desperately wanted to help her, so I did some praying, some brainstorming, some research, some interviewing, and this chapter was born.

Why a "Normal" Guy Wouldn't Want Sex

One of the people I asked for advice was my husband. "What could be some reasons why a guy would never want to have sex with his wife?" I wanted to know.

"There's something wrong with a guy who never wants sex," he replied. So he wasn't much help. Actually, after some thought he did come up with some of the ideas you see here:

- He's too tired.
- He's afraid he won't be able to perform.
- He has guilt left over from premarital sex.
- He's afraid of getting his wife pregnant.
- He's not attracted to his wife.
- Work takes up all his time.
- He has control issues.
- He's bothered by his wife's sexual past.
- He fears emotional rejection.
- There are problems in the marriage.
- He's involved with pornography.
- He's having an affair.

I'm sure this list, which I'll explore in the following pages, is not exhaustive, but if your husband is never "in the mood," then maybe something will catch your attention as a possible reason why. Please don't jump to conclusions, though. Just because "pornography" and "he's not attracted to his wife" made the list does *not* mean that they apply to *your* husband. Some men may be able to relate to several factors on the list. For others, it may just be one. There's also a very real possibility that your husband's particular problem is something not listed.

Paul must have known there were men like Anne's husband, or he wouldn't have commanded, in his first letter to the Corinthians, *both* women and men not to withhold sex from their marriage partner. "The husband should fulfill his marital duty to his wife, and likewise the wife to her husband." He could have singled out the ladies but didn't.

So why might a normal guy not want sex? Let's look at some possible options.

He's too tired. Fatigue is a very real inhibitor when it comes to a healthy sex life. Usually, women are the ones who are too tired for sex (especially moms). But depending on what your husband does all day and how much sleep he gets, fatigue can be a big problem for him, too. A man who is extremely tired may not have the energy to achieve and maintain an erection—even if sex sounds like fun to him at the time. Sex takes a lot out of a man physically, and if he's drained before he even begins, he could be in trouble.

Ideas if this is a habit: get more sleep, cut back hours at work, get a less physically demanding job, exercise in the morning instead of right before bed, eat fewer carbohydrates, take a power nap right after work.

If your husband is exhausted as a rule, pray about what you can do to help him find some more energy.

He's afraid he won't be able to perform. Like we've talked about before, a huge chunk of a man's identity and self-worth is wrapped up in his sexual performance. If he has had trouble performing up to par in the past, the fear of repeat problems could be enough to keep him celibate.

We all naturally shy away from activities we're not good at. The fear of failure can be daunting—particularly the fear of impotence. He desperately wants to please you, to meet your sexual needs. If he's physically unable, this can be emotionally crushing.

If he's concerned that his penis isn't large enough to satisfy you, assure him that is not the case. Studies show that even the shortest penis is big enough to pleasure a woman during sex.

Perhaps your husband has low testosterone levels or struggles with clinical depression. Maybe he is overstressed and it is affecting him physically. Maybe he has erectile dysfunction.

If you think your husband's problem might fit in the physical category, gently encourage him to get some help. Assure him that he's no less of a man for needing a little intervention. Tell him you're proud of him for doing the best thing for you both.

He has guilt left over from premarital sex. Soon after Anne told me about her husband's lack of interest in sex, my friend Julia felt emboldened to share her similar story.

After some discussion, we concluded that these friends had two key things in common: 1) They both had sex with their husbands before they were married; and 2) both of these men were raised in strict Christian homes. There's no telling what their parents would have done if they knew. They still don't know.

I asked Anne and Julia if they thought there could be a connection there. The guilt could be overwhelming these guys. They thought it was definitely possible.

Julia also mentioned that the sex she and her husband had in his sports car *before* they were married was a lot hotter than the sex they infrequently had now—four kids and two minivans later.

If you had sex before your wedding, you know that once you're married, the "forbidden fruit," deliciously naughty aspect of sex is gone. You'll have to retrain your minds to enjoy the sex you're having now.

And like we talked about in chapter 4, guilt over the past can be a real inhibitor to lovemaking in the present. Pray that your husband will look to the Lord for forgiveness and truly believe Christ's blood has made him completely clean.

Encourage him to take a look at the life of David, a man who committed terrible sexual sin—and then kept on sinning. Not only did God forgive David and make him clean, He called him "a man after God's own heart."

"Blessed is he whose transgressions are forgiven, whose sins are covered," writes David himself in Psalm 32. "Blessed is the man whose sin the Lord does not count against him."

He's afraid of his wife getting pregnant. I'm not sure how common this reason is. I know many women shy away from sex when they're afraid of becoming pregnant. A couple who are friends of ours tried natural family planning the first year of their marriage and became pregnant four years before they'd planned. The wife used more effective methods of birth control from then on, scared to death of another unplanned pregnancy. If she was even five minutes late taking her pill one morning, no sex for at least three days.

If you've gotten pregnant before without meaning to, or if your husband is concerned about providing for children, or if he just doesn't feel ready to be a dad, the fear of you conceiving a baby could be very real to him.

Do some research on birth-control options together. An educated decision might help ease your husband's mind. You might even consider "doubling up" on methods—say a condom *and* spermicide.

Some women get pregnant on the sly, pretending to take their pills or lying about when they're ovulating. Don't ever do this. Your husband needs to know he can trust you.

He's not attracted to his wife. First of all, let me say that the handful of women I know whose husbands don't want sex are beautiful women. Gorgeous even. Any hot-blooded man would think so. And I know husbands who ask for sex all the time from their less-than-average-looking wives. If your husband doesn't want sex, don't immediately assume you're ugly!

That said, if your husband claims that he's not attracted to you, the first order of business is to figure out why. Has your appearance changed drastically in the months or years since you got married? Have you gained a lot of weight or failed to take care of yourself? Have you neglected to make sure you look and smell clean?

Or is your husband letting his eyes wander to other women and comparing you unfavorably (and unfairly) to 18-year-old airbrushed supermodels? Is he fantasizing about women he's seen on porn sites?

If you're a reasonably attractive woman who takes moderately good care of yourself, your husband should still want to have sex with you. If he wanted to before, and *you* haven't changed, then *he's* the one who has.

If neither of you are happy with your appearance, pray for the strength to make some necessary changes—and then do your best to become the woman you know you can be.

Work takes up all his time. Men naturally feel a responsibility to provide for their families. For some men, this burden is heavier than for others. If your husband's father was extremely successful at his work, your husband may feel extra pressure as the family breadwinner. If your husband feels insecure in one or more areas of his life, he may throw himself into his work even more in an attempt to prove his worth. Making money often produces a sense of power which can become addicting. Soon, nothing feels as good to him as closing a deal or making a big sale or stockpiling overtime pay.

I have a couple friends whose husbands could be labeled workaholics. They find their worth in their work, and it often leaves little time, energy, or desire for anything (or anyone) else. Sex is merely an unwelcome distraction on their fast and furious climb to the top.

When these couples do have sex, it's always at the same time on the same day of the week—merely one more item on the husband's strict schedule or crammed to-do list.

Pray that God will give you the words to say to your husband—non-offensive words that affirm his worth in your eyes apart from his work. Without criticizing him, let him know that spending time with him is far more important to you than more money. Ask God to convict him that his priorities need rearranged.

He has control issues. People who struggle with control issues and trusting their mate often have a hard time achieving orgasm. They're always on guard, afraid to be vulnerable, afraid of abandoning themselves to their mates.

The act of sex involves getting lost in the moment, losing control. If this scares your husband, he could decide it's easier to just avoid sex altogether.

Control issues often stem from feeling *out* of control in some past situation. Pray that God will help your husband resolve those issues so your marriage doesn't suffer needlessly.

He's bothered by his wife's sexual past. If you had a sexual history before you met your husband, and he didn't, this could cause some problems. Picturing you with another man in an intimate situation could be very hard on him. He might worry that you're thinking of someone else while making love to him.

Perhaps he has lost respect for you or looks at you as "damaged goods." One wife told me her husband said, "I feel like you've been all used up." This crushed her.

Love your husband without reserve. Shower him with affection. Focus on *him, his* body, *his* feelings. Do everything in your power to show him you're completely in love with *him* and no one else. What's past is past.

Just as God has completely forgiven you if you've asked Him to, your husband should be willing to do the same. It won't be easy for him to do, but you can pray that God will give him the strength.

He fears emotional rejection. Sex is more than physical for a man. He becomes incredibly vulnerable emotionally when he makes love to his wife. Has your husband been emotionally wounded or rejected in the past by someone he loved? Was it *you*?

He may fear getting close to you because he feels he's just setting himself up to get hurt. Some men can get past the emotional rejection and keep coming back to ask for more sex. Others completely shut down emotionally. Could this be your husband?

What are some ways you could better meet his emotional needs? What are some things he needs to see or hear from you in order to feel loved? If you don't know, ask him to share, to open himself up. This could take time. Maybe he needs some nonsexual needs met before he's ready for sex.

If you have rejected your husband in the past, ask for forgiveness. Ask him how you can show him that you won't ever do it again. Then set out to prove that you mean what you say.

There are problems in the marriage. Sex aside, how is the rest of your marriage? Are there issues with respect? Is there unresolved conflict? Ongoing conflict can be a real sex-extinguisher—putting out the flames of passion before they even have a chance to get going.

How would you characterize your overall relationship with your husband? Lots of arguing and fighting? Who generally starts it? Is there anything you can do to lessen the tension between the two of you?

It's not easy to extend grace to your husband when he doesn't deserve it, but think of how often God does that for us. It means letting go of the need to be right all the time—not an easy task for us gals.

If you are contributing to your marital problems, pray that God will help you change your attitude and actions. Don't sabotage your sex life if you want your marriage to survive! As one of the proverbs warns us, "The wise woman builds her house, but with her own hands the foolish one tears hers down." Don't be a foolish wife!

Some problems can be solved with prayer and some honest communication. Other problems may need the help of a Christian counselor, pastor, or trusted friend.

Do whatever it takes to resolve any issues that are standing in the way of a satisfying sex life.

Not Easy, but Possible

Dr. Tim Gardner says, "Husbands and wives who desire to create a marriage that fully enters into the mystery of holy sex must fight together against the deadly intrusion of pornography, and they must fight in prayer and love...With prayer, accountability, and the power of God, pornography addiction can be overcome."

He's involved with pornography. Men get tangled up in pornography for many different reasons. And viewing porn typically involves masturbation. A man who is frequently finding sexual release on his own isn't going to want or need sex from his wife.

If you discover that your husband has a problem with porn (and you're not alone!), get help.

Many men don't see the problem with pornography—or so they say. "I do it alone. It's not hurting anyone," they reason. Well, it is. It's hurting them—and it's hurting their wives. When a husband looks at porn, he's telling his wife that she's not enough, that she's inadequate to meet his needs.

And for a man involved in porn, his wife *isn't* enough. His appetite becomes more and more insatiable, and his wife can't compete.

He's having an affair. The only thing more crushing than discovering that your husband is addicted to porn is finding out that he is involved in an adulterous affair. Don't jump to conclusions on this one. Give your husband the benefit of the doubt—at least initially. Explore other reasons from this chapter first. Trust your husband until he gives you a good reason not to.

If you do find out that your husband has committed adultery, it's imperative that you seek godly counseling if your marriage is to be saved.

What Can You Do?

Your sexual relationship with your husband is worth fighting for. So, how are you going to go about it?

The first step is to pray. Acknowledge the fact that, as Jesus tells us, "Apart from me you can do nothing." Take this all-important matter to God and ask Him how He'd like you to pursue the solution to your problem. Ask Him to show you when and how to approach your husband and what steps you can take in the meantime. Ask one or two godly women you trust to uphold you in prayer as well.

When God gives you the go-ahead, lovingly communicate your concerns to your husband. Don't hit him over the head with Scriptures that declare his obligation to you. Don't point fingers or get defensive. Don't compare him to other men, ask him what his problem is, or make threats.

Reassure him that you love him, that you're committed to this marriage, and that you want to do whatever you can to restore an awesome sex life. Reaffirm who he is as a man. Share some of his traits you admire.

Be gentle. Take it slow. And bathe every word you say in prayer. Ask your husband what he would like you to do as a first step toward resolving this problem in your marriage.

Hopefully, he'll be responsive, open, and willing to change and get help. If so, move forward in whatever direction you decide together.

If not, drop the matter and spend more time with the Lord in prayer. If you've never read it, I highly recommend Stormie Omartian's *The Power of a Praying Wife.* "The joy of seeing something hopelessly dead brought to life is the greatest joy we can know," Stormie says. "The power that resurrected Jesus is the very same power that will resurrect the dead places of your marriage and put life back into it."

As difficult as it may seem at first, "Be strong and take heart and wait for the LORD," as Psalm 27 encourages us. And trust Him to answer in His perfect timing.

THE
POWER OF
THE MIND

Chapter 7

Sex Drawers
and Such

I t's all in our heads. Sexual desire, that is. We women sometimes lament our lack of desire as if we're helpless to increase it. Like we've got to sit around and wait to have it bestowed upon us.

News flash: There is no libido fairy. And we have more control over our sex drives than we think—"think" being the operative word.

The mind really is a powerful thing, a terrible thing to waste, and all that. As has been said, "Beware of what you set your mind on, for that you will surely become."

In other words, set your mind on a passionate sexual relationship with your husband, and it will (eventually, with a healthy dose of hard work and prayer) happen!

A prime example: When I began my "research" for this book, my sexual desire went soaring off the charts—off my normal, everyday charts anyway. As I read and researched sex books, an interesting thing happened—I was much more enthused about making love.

For a while there, Gabe would grin every time I walked out into his home office—especially when the girls were napping or watching a DVD—because he was wondering whether I was there to whisk him away to the bedroom yet again.

When you've got sex on the brain, you're more likely to want it in the flesh. In fact, several women told me that just filling out the survey for this book made them hungry for sex.

Anybody want a survey?

Win the Battle of the Mind

So we know how mental and emotional sex is for us women. It's hard for us to get turned on if the emotional atmosphere in our marriage isn't "just so." Maybe if our husbands were romantic, caring, and thoughtful 100 percent of the time (and the rest of our lives were running smoothly!), we wouldn't have any problem desiring sex.

When our husbands do things that turn us off emotionally, our physical switches flip off too. We can either try to change our husbands (impossible) or find a way to disconnect our emotional and physical switches from each other (also impossible).

A better choice is to retrain our brains. Rewire our minds to choose a loving attitude. Be willing to have sex even when the circumstances are not ideal.

Our husbands may try to turn us on, but it will never happen if we don't *want* to be turned on. The physical part of us can rarely be won over when the mental part of us is fighting it like a tiger.

The battle over sex—essentially the battle for our marriages—is won or lost in our heads. We have the power to consciously choose to do the loving thing. Let me rephrase that—*God* has the power and promises it can be ours for the asking.

We can ask for things we don't really want, you know. We just have to ask for the *desire* for what we're requesting, right along with the request.

In other words, don't wait until you *want* to be unselfish and loving and *then* ask God to help you out. Everything inside of you may be screaming, "I hate my husband and don't ever want to love him!" That's the perfect time to ask God, "Please, Lord, help me *want* to love my husband. I know it's what I need to do, but it's honestly the last thing I feel like doing right now. I can't believe I'm even asking You!"

Once you've prayed, there are other practical things you can do while you wait for God to answer.

You can read about sex. Think sexual thoughts about your husband. Imagine sexy scenarios involving the two of you. Invest time and thought and energy into physical and mental preparation for sex. Learn as much as you can about him and what makes him tick.

The more you think about your husband in a sexual way, the more fun you'll have making love.

I like to apply a verse from Philippians 4 to sex. As *The Message* puts it,

> You'll do best by filling your minds and meditating on things true, noble, reputable, authentic, compelling, gracious—the best, not the worst; the beautiful, not the ugly; things to praise, not things to curse.

Fantasize about your hubby and things you've done in the past. Remind yourself of how good sex can be. Write about your experiences in a safely kept journal. Read back through it to jog your memory. Remembering in detail a certain sexual experience with your husband might create the longing to experience it once again.

And get busy adding different experiences to your repertoire, so you'll have something to reflect back on—and re-create—later.

There are times when we're making love that I think, or even say to Gabe, "Why in the world don't we do this *every* night?" Or three or four times a day, for that matter!

So, why, when bedtime rolls around the next night, do I forget just how delicious that experience was? Why am I not dying to re-create the previous night's encounter? Don't wait until you forget how good the performance was before you go for an encore.

There is absolutely nothing wrong with training your mind to think sexual thoughts—of your *husband*. Sex is so much better when you're longing for your husband long before you slip into bed.

God gave us our minds. He expects that we will use them. Wisely.

And that *we* will control *them,* not the other way around. That we will take every thought captive to make it obedient to Christ.

Take a Walk Around the Closet

There are a lot of great sex analogies out there. Men are like microwaves; women are like Crock-Pots. Men are like lightbulbs; women are like irons.

But my all-time favorite (courtesy of Karen Linamen) draws a parallel between sex and familiar bedroom furnishings—dressers and walk-in closets. Can you guess which one matches each gender?

Men tend to compartmentalize their life into separate drawers—a drawer for work, a drawer for play, a drawer for the kids, a drawer for the wife, a drawer for sex. (Remember that crazy testosterone bath they got in utero?)

We women, on the other hand, cannot divide our lives into neat and tidy parts. Just like a walk-in closet, it's all there in front of us all the time. We find it virtually impossible to focus on just one thing at once. All the parts of our lives—job, family, friends, church, hobbies, finances—mesh together into one big, integrated, complicated whole.

When it's time to take a tumble in the sheets, men merely open their sex drawer, slam the others shut, and they're ready to roll. It doesn't matter what the final score of the basketball game was or how hectic tomorrow's schedule is—those drawers are closed. For guys, it's out of sight, out of mind.

Women have no sex drawer. Sex is sitting on a wide-open shelf in the walk-in closet, right beside the bills due tomorrow, the looming laundry pile, and the milk you meant to pick up at the grocery.

Not to mention the squabble you and a co-worker got into that morning, the argument you and your husband had over dinner, and the fact that your sister hasn't returned any of your phone calls in over a week.

Even if your "closet" is neat and completely organized, you are simply incapable of looking at one item without seeing all the rest.

I don't know about you, but for me, having an orgasm is next to impossible if I'm not in the moment. I have to be completely focused on my husband and what our bodies are doing, or I don't stand a chance. And the older I get, the more kids I have, and the fuller my life becomes, the harder it gets.

Men typically see sex as a stress reliever. Bad day? No problem. Just have sex.

We women have a hard time with sex when we're emotionally, physically or mentally overwhelmed. Bad day? Big problem. Can't focus on sex.

A Simple Solution

So what is a girl to do? I don't claim to have found "the answer," but I do have a suggestion.

Ideally, you will have such a loving, adoring relationship with your spouse and enough time to do romantic things together all evening long that getting in the mood will hardly be an issue for you.

In the event, however, that you find yourself running around like crazy all day and into the evening and feel like making love about as much as you feel like getting pinkeye...here's an idea.

Pretend you're somewhere else. Not with *someone* else. But *somewhere* else. Pretend you and your husband are naked on a beach or in the woods, making love and praying no one comes along and sees you. You can even play a nature sounds CD of waves crashing against the shore or birds chirping in the forest to help set the mood. (I recently bought one of each at Wal-Mart for a dollar apiece.)

If you're feeling extra-adventurous, you could always pour sand on your sheets or haul in tree branches from the backyard to fill your bed, but I wouldn't necessarily recommend it.

Not a big fan of the great outdoors? Pretend you're at a party and you and your husband can't wait until you get home, so you sneak upstairs, tear off each other's clothes, and make love in one of the bedrooms. Or you're at a business conference at a hotel and you slip out during a meeting for an afternoon tryst in your room.

Let me explain my logic behind suggesting an imaginary change of scenery. I can't compartmentalize my life into separate drawers, and I can't walk into that gigantic closet known as "my life" and have sex without thinking of a million other things. So I have to get out of the closet, out of my home, and into another place. A place where nothing exists but my husband and me. No job. No kids. No bills. No in-laws. No stress.

People read romance novels as an escape from their daily lives. Plop yourself and your hubby down into your own little mini-romance novel. Escape from your day. Get far, far away. To the beach. The woods. The party. The hotel.

I love it when one of our moms keeps our girls overnight, and Gabe and I are able to get away on a date and come home to an empty house. Times like these, it doesn't take any fantasizing on my part to get (and stay) aroused during lovemaking. The mood has already been set, we've enjoyed each other's company in public, and now we're ready to enjoy

Case in Point

I remember one night when Gabe and I made love during intermission of a playoff hockey game. Romantic, I know. I had spent the hour prior paying our bills and analyzing our finances. I was a little stressed. At the beginning of the game, we'd made a "date" for intermission but I hadn't realized how quickly it would approach. I wasn't ready.

As we climbed into bed, I told Gabe, "I'll just warn you. I have facts and figures swirling around in my head, and I don't know if I can jump right into lovemaking mode."

"Just don't think about that stuff," was his male-minded advice.

I let out an exasperated sigh and gave him a 45-second speech on the "men are dresser drawers" analogy. He still didn't get it.

So I went with Plan B. "Let's pretend we're somewhere else," I suggested. "Where do you want to go?"

We started giggling as we came up with some half-baked ideas and joked around while we cuddled. The good news was that the whole event was a huge success, and we both decided to mentally stay in our bedroom.

Imagine that—great sex without even going to the beach!

each other privately. No need to escape to the beach when our own bedroom is hot and steamy!

Again, ideally, you'll be mentally ready for sex at all times—your day will go perfectly, your husband will be completely romantic and angelic at all times, and life will be rosy.

But, for that "rare" time when you've had a rough day and you just can't get in the mood, fantasize that you and your hubby are in a different place and under different circumstances. The possibilities are endless.

Another Alternative

If you don't feel comfortable letting your imagination run wild, try this instead. Plan a lovemaking date with your husband 24 hours in advance, and then spend a few minutes every couple hours mentally preparing for sex. Yes, it will require a time commitment—and we're all just sooo busy. But think of it as a high-return investment. Here are a few activities that can help:

- Some of your time can be spent in prayer, asking God to help you clear your mind and focus on making love. You can spend some time relaxing—maybe even taking a soak in the tub so your muscles aren't tense and you're not wound too tight.

- Find something sexy to wear. Wear lingerie under your clothes all day long if you can. My friend Daphne wears a thong to work on the days she and her husband have planned to make love. It makes her feel sexy all day long (without anyone else noticing) and ready to roll that evening.

- "I take a nice warm shower," Liz says. "Even when I'm exhausted, a warm shower always makes me feel better. I always shower before bed. I like to feel clean and fresh." If you don't shower, at least brush your teeth and freshen up your makeup. Make sure your legs are shaved and spritz on a bit of your hubby's favorite perfume.

- Cuddle for a while ahead of time or watch a romantic comedy together. Spend time unwinding with a good book prior to making love. A Christian book about sex would make a great choice. I like *Sheet Music* by Dr. Kevin Leman, *Pillow Talk* by Karen Linamen, and *Red-Hot Monogamy* by Bill and Pam Farrel. Reading about sex is a big turn-on.

Jumping straight from bills and laundry to bed just doesn't work. Remember, God didn't give us women dressers with easy-shut drawers. We're the ones with the big, open closets. So, make the best of it, and take some time to set the mood in your walk-in. Light some candles. Play a CD of love songs or instrumental music. Read that sex book.

You've got to engage your mind—get your head in the game. And that often means purposefully thinking about sex all throughout the day.

My friend Holly takes the matter of sex to the Lord in prayer before she goes to her husband. "I start by praying to be submissive to both my heavenly Father and my husband," she says. "I remember that men need sex about every three days. Also, it will bring us closer and keep him satisfied, making it easier for him to guard his heart. And I ask him to make me in the mood! Oh, yeah! Also, the kids or whatever is on my mind can wait and will be fine until we are done. But he won't until we are done!"

Good sex often takes a lot of time and preparation. Your husband, like we've talked about, will rarely need all that, but you probably do. Most of the time we just don't want to make the effort. But it's an investment of time you won't regret.

Remember when you first started dating your husband? You put the rest of the world on hold. Nothing mattered but your beloved. These days, your beloved is the only thing on hold, and everything else in your life is just so *extremely* important…

That has *got* to change, my friend.

Your Assignment—Should You Choose to Accept It

You can do it. I have faith in you. We'll do it together.

Here's your homework: When you wake up tomorrow morning, talk to your husband and set a time for making love. At least one full hour before that time, finish up every loose end of what you've been working on that evening—pay the last bill, turn your computer off, close your book and put it away, whatever.

Make sure hubby doesn't get any ideas about starting ahead of schedule—let him know it will be in his best interest to wait!

Let's say your task wrap-up takes half an hour. Use the remaining 30 minutes wisely by doing some of the things we talked about before. Brush your teeth, freshen up (maybe even take a bath or shower), and slip into some lingerie. Fold back the covers on your bed, prop up your pillows, turn on some sexy music, light a candle, and find a Christian sex book to browse. Ask God to bless your time with your husband and give you the ability to focus and even climax.

If hubby is willing, ask that he take a quick shower, splash on some cologne, and enter the room wearing silk boxers, or whatever turns you on.

By the time he comes to bed, you might *already* be turned on, thinking about sex and greatly anticipating his arrival. No more "agonizing" foreplay where you "just know" you're not going to get aroused, let alone make it to orgasm.

Oh, you can still have foreplay, but it will be filled with desire, not dread—appetite, not apprehension. Your hubby won't have to spend long and torturous minutes hoping to turn you on and not even knowing if it will work.

I should probably take a moment to insert a tiny disclaimer and remind you that life does not always go as planned. Things will occasionally come up that will threaten to ruin your prep time or lovemaking experience—a crying child, telephone emergency, a nasty case of the sniffles. Just do your best, don't give up hope, and try again another night.

But inconvenient disruptions aside, being mentally prepared makes a world of difference and will change the tune of your lovemaking entirely.

You won't have to make this effort every single time you make love. Sometimes it simply won't be necessary. You know yourself and your body. You know the mood you're in at the moment. You'll know when you need to go that extra mile.

Going the extra mile is just like it sounds—hard, extra work when you're already tired. Do it anyway, or you'll wish you had.

When it's all said and done, and we're both happily snuggled under the sheets, I've never regretted walking that extra mile. You won't either.

Chapter 8

Are Orgasms Overrated?

don't know where you stand when it comes to the Big O. You could be anywhere on the orgasm spectrum. Maybe you've had hundreds of them. Or maybe you can count them on one hand. Maybe you've never experienced one. Or maybe you're like the game Battleship—a hit followed by seven misses, two more hits, then six misses, another hit…

We're going to spend some quality time talking about orgasms and trying to figure them out, because they're awfully important. And awfully fun. If you're not regularly having them, you and your husband probably feel like something is missing in your sex life.

Are orgasms overrated? In a way, perhaps. Yes, you can still enjoy sex without reaching orgasm. A sexual experience without a climax is not a "failure." Sex is a complete and intimate experience, not just a mindless race to a goal. As Tim Alan Gardner stresses, *oneness,* not orgasm, should be the goal of sex.

That said, orgasms are still a fabulous frosting on the proverbial sexual cake.

Some women won't regularly orgasm until they've had lots of experience with sex. For some women, it takes more than just experience. They have to put forth a lot of time and effort.

A study was conducted not too long ago that concluded that women in their 20s are least likely to achieve orgasm, while women in their 40s have the best and most orgasms. Now that should give you hope! If you're struggling in this area, you're not staring down a perpetually black-as-night tunnel. There is light up ahead! (Not that you have to sit back and wait for your fortieth birthday!)

Before I got married and had sex, I honestly thought that orgasms would come completely naturally to me. I subconsciously expected them to materialize out of thin air with a wave of my magic wand.

Ha! I now know that orgasms are 90 percent (if not 99 percent) mental. (Not that I have a scientific study to back up my numbers—just my personal opinion.) The point is, you really do have to *learn* how to have an orgasm, as crazy and unsexy as that seems.

I hope to help you as much as I can, but as your "teacher," I must warn you that the final exam will not be multiple-choice. It will be a practical-application-of-skills exam. As a good student, you will have to do more than read this chapter once through—you'll have to put in some hours studying. And more importantly, *practicing*.

My Favorite Part

Fortunately, this isn't a sex textbook. I won't bore you with talk of scrotums and vulvas. But if you lack the necessary basic knowledge of our sexual parts and how God put them together, don't be afraid to read up on the topic. It does help to know how your husband's body—and your own—work.*

I do want to talk a little about parts for a moment, though—one special part in particular. My personal favorite. You're probably already aware of the fact that we women have a body part that serves one solitary purpose—allowing us to experience sexual pleasure.

---

* *Intended for Pleasure* by Ed and Gaye Wheat has a chapter entitled "Understanding the Basics" that explains sexual fundamentals with helpful diagrams. Other books like *The Act of Marriage* by Tim and Beverly LaHaye and *A Celebration of Sex* by Douglas Rosenau do, too. Don't hesitate to check one of them out.

Our breasts are sexual but are also good for nursing babies. Our vaginas are sexual but also used for birthing those suckling babes.

But what about the clitoris? It's a hard one to describe. I like to think of it as *simply magic*. Located just beneath the flesh, above the opening to the urethra and vagina, the clitoris does nothing all day but help bring you to orgasm.

Let me rephrase that. The only job the clitoris has is stimulating orgasm. She has no other marketable skills to speak of. When she's not

The Love Muscle

Did you know you have "love muscles" you can easily exercise to help you become more orgasmic? Your pubococcygeus (PC) muscles, the same muscles that stop your urine flow, can also be used to squeeze your husband's penis during sex, providing better friction for both of you and helping him feel "tighter."

Other perks of exercising these muscles? After giving birth, they can help tighten your vaginal muscles back up. They can also help you become more orgasmic, getting your private parts ready for making love.

A PC "workout" is as simple as placing one finger in your vagina and squeezing it over and over again. Or, if that doesn't appeal to you, you can practice on the toilet by actually stopping your urine flow. Start, stop, start, stop.

These exercises (called Kegel exercises) can actually be done anywhere—your desk at work, the kitchen sink, standing in line at Wal-Mart—once you figure out where your PC muscles are and how to flex them. No fingers or toilets necessary. Just squeeze them for a few seconds (as if you're stopping your urine flow), 10 times at first, and work up to more. (Just be sure you've mastered a poker face of sorts before you try them in public. It could make for some embarrassing situations.)

You'll probably find that Kegels get the blood flowing in your most private parts and send messages to your brain that you're ready for action. Do them next time you're in the car on the way home to your husband to put you in the mood for sex!

busy with orgasms, she's out of work—and virtually unemployable. This body part has no other function whatsoever.

Amazing to think about. God designed each of your body parts with a specific function and purpose in mind, and He gave you a part created *exclusively* for enjoying your sexuality.

In fact, some researchers believe—and I agree—that there is no such thing as a vaginal orgasm, and that the clitoris must be stimulated in some way for you to experience those tidal waves of pleasure.

Some women view sex as a duty. They think of themselves merely as the means for their husbands to achieve sexual expression and release. "God didn't create me to receive pleasure but to give it to my husband," they say, with their best martyr accent. But that can't be true—not when God gave you a clitoris! You are more than just a vagina!

Yes, God absolutely created your body to give your husband sexual pleasure, but He meant for *you* to experience it, too. And your husband's sexual desires include *your* fulfillment and enjoyment—that turns him on!

A Touchy Subject

Many godly men and women have written wonderful books on sex that include sections on self-discovery—touching your own genitals to learn what feels best to you. When I read something like this for the first time, I immediately thought, "Oh my! That's masturbation! How can that be okay?"

The Bible is silent on the subject of touching yourself, and masturbation is most commonly associated with dirty magazines and phone sex or the like. These activities are addictive and wrong. But that's not the kind of touching these books are talking about. Let me share with you some thoughts from Dr. Kevin Leman's book *Sheet Music* and invite you to think them through for yourself.

He encourages women to pamper themselves with a long, hot bath and some candles. And then, yes, start touching yourself to find out what feels good. Find out how your clitoris likes to be rubbed. Take your time and explore. You might feel less pressure without your husband there, waiting for his own orgasm.

Some women (and men) may be tempted to use masturbation as a way to avoid intimacy with their spouse. They achieve orgasm on their own and forego sex with their mates. This is wrong! The Bible tells us specifically not to withhold ourselves from our husbands (and wives).

But when you are learning to respond to your husband so that you can have a richer, more satisfying sexual experience, you're working toward greater intimacy. You're training yourself to become a better lover for him.

If touching yourself makes you uncomfortable, or you feel it is wrong, *don't do it*. Dr. Leman suggests asking your husband if he will experiment with you in a no-pressure-to-orgasm time of exploring your genitals and what feels good to you.

Assure your husband that his patience and understanding will be handsomely rewarded once you figure out what makes you go.

Did I Have One or Not?

I've had a couple women comment to me that they aren't really sure if they've experienced an orgasm or not. This is understandable. For a guy, there's no mistaking an orgasm for something else. The physical evidence speaks for itself.

For a woman, it's not quite so black-and-white. You might feel like your desire is rising higher and higher and higher and then—*pow!*—it's over, and you're not sure if you actually climaxed. Maybe you feel a little wave of pleasure, but nothing like the big breakers and whitecaps you were expecting.

The best gauge for knowing whether or not you actually reached orgasm is how you feel when you're done making love. If your body feels frustrated, tense, or balled-up inside, you probably didn't. If on the other hand, you feel relaxed and free—like you've just released a load of tension—you more than likely had an orgasm.

I certainly can't speak for all men, but when I asked my husband, he said that orgasms basically feel the same every time for him. Wonderful, but the same.

For women, no two orgasms are alike. They vary in length, intensity, and overall feeling. And we women are completely capable of teetering on the edge of orgasm, getting distracted, and having it fizzle out and die. So, it's easy to see why you might not always recognize one when it happens.

With time, you'll hopefully experience such mind-blowing orgasms that there won't even be a question of "Did I or didn't I?" There won't be a shred of doubt in your mind—or your husband's.

Positions that Work

When it comes to having an orgasm, for some women, position is everything. Since it is necessary for the clitoris to be indirectly, if not directly, stimulated for a woman to achieve orgasm, the position you choose must take that into account.

My personal opinion—and you are more than welcome to have yours—is that wife-on-top is the best position for a successful orgasm.

Lana agrees. "We always start out sex with me on top," she says. "Well, after foreplay, I mean. I can move exactly how I need to in order to feel it on my clitoris. Sometimes I lay down flat against my husband. Sometimes I prop myself up with my hands and knees. And sometimes I even lean backward. He fondles my nipples, my rear end, or whatever else I ask him to. I can kiss him or not. And move as fast or slow as I want. Up, down, in, out, back, and forth. It works almost every time, and then when I'm done, we have sex however he wants. We're perfectly happy with the arrangement."

If you're trying—and failing—to achieve orgasm in the missionary position (husband on top), you're not alone. Unless you slip a pillow under your pelvis, or find a way to maneuver your body so your clitoris is stimulated, your main sexual organ is probably going to be sitting on the sidelines.

Depending on the position of your bodies, your husband may be able to stroke your clitoris with his fingers even while he's inside you. If direct stimulation is uncomfortable, especially at first, gently move your husband's hand to a spot where your clitoris can be indirectly caressed.

At the Same Time

While orgasms may not be overrated, *simultaneous* orgasms are. You know—where you both erupt in a thunderous release of passion and pleasure at the same time. Don't get me wrong. Synchronized orgasms can be fabulous—a special time of connection between you and your hubby. But don't kill yourself trying to make one happen.

Seriously. You don't need to be stressing over it—unless it's extremely important to your husband. Then give it your best shot. But it can be detrimental to your sexual experience if you attempt the simultaneous and botch it up. It's a risky move with a low percentage of success—especially for beginners.

The pressure on you to "go off" at a precise time can be nerve-racking and can work against your ability to relax and orgasm. And if hubby gets there before you do, there's no turning back for him, and you'll be left with a limp penis.

My suggestion is to make it your goal for hubby to focus on your orgasm first, and once that is completed, he's free to concentrate on his own release. Just make sure to be an unselfish lover and stay excited for him even after you've had your fun. I know that can be hard.

"I got what I came for," you say to yourself with a contented sigh. "Now back to that book I was reading!" Stay in the zone, girl. You owe it to your hubby.

Once you get good at orgasms, then you can try to do it together. You might know—or be—a couple that regularly climaxes together. That's awesome.

But for a majority of people, coinciding orgasms are not a reality, and that's perfectly okay.

Dr. Leman makes a point I hadn't really considered. He reminds us women that most men get more pleasure out of watching their wives orgasm than experiencing it themselves. So, he doesn't put much stock in the synchronized ones. It doesn't happen that often with him and his wife, he says, and "when it does occur, frankly, I feel like I'm missing out. I'm so caught up in what I'm experiencing that I don't get to see all that Sande is enjoying."

Bottom line? If your hubby wants to try it, give it a whirl. If he'd rather watch you first, then by all means, go right ahead!

Don't Succumb to Laziness

I'm not pointing any fingers at you that I'm not also pointing at myself, but I think one of the biggest obstacles to orgasm is our own laziness. We aren't quite the sexual creatures our husbands are, and orgasm for us doesn't come as easily. Since we don't need sex as much as they do, we don't see the point in putting forth all that effort.

That's lazy. And selfish.

If we're not in the mood, we say, "Sorry, honey, I'm just not in the mood." What we should be doing is *getting in the mood*. And getting in the mood can take some effort.

A woman simply cannot reach orgasm if she's not mentally and emotionally in the moment. Your husband can touch you in all the right ways in all the right places, but if you're upset about something, or distracted, or you just don't feel like making love, there will be no orgasm.

"I just can't have an orgasm," my friend Jenny told me, obviously frustrated. "Dave wants to try new positions so that I'll be able to experience one, but each night I usually say, 'You go ahead, honey. Maybe next time for me.' It's always 'next time' and it never happens."

I can certainly relate to this! There have been many times in eight years of marriage that I just couldn't orgasm, no matter how hard I tried. But quite a few times I had no desire to even try.

If you've been trying for a good part of an hour and have tried everything in the book, and still can't orgasm, don't be tempted to fake it. Just tell your husband honestly, "I'm just not feeling it tonight, honey. You go ahead." But don't do this more than occasionally. I think it should be an exception, not a rule.

Now, if you're trying your darnedest to experience an orgasm regularly, or just to experience one at all, then I commend you. If you desperately want to please your husband and give him the pleasure of bringing you to orgasm, but you rarely, if ever, experience a climax during lovemaking, then laziness is not your problem.

Making It Better

If a doctor has assured you there's nothing physically wrong with you (and the failure to orgasm is rarely a physical problem), here are a couple helpful hints.

First, pray about it. Tell God that you want to be sexually fulfilled, for your husband, as well as yourself. Ask Him to give you wisdom, desire, patience, and perseverance as you make your way over this hurdle.

Then talk to your husband. Tell him that you want to experience orgasms, because you know it will greatly enhance your sex life and your marriage. Tell him that you are committed to doing whatever you can to achieve this. Encourage him to be patient with you as you strive for this goal.

Try some of the suggestions in this chapter. Learn more about your body by reading up on the basics of sex. Exercise your PC muscles. Take some time for self-discovery—find out what feels good to you. Try a new position, like wife on top. If it doesn't work right away, try different variations. Don't worry about simultaneous orgasms—you go first!

And while you're making love, for goodness sake, help your hubby out! Gently tell him when something feels nice and when it doesn't feel so great. Point him in the right direction. Guide his hands and his mouth. He can't read your mind—and though he can read your body to some degree, there's always more to learn. You aren't insulting him by helping him—he'll be grateful.

Building Trust on Both Sides

I've had a couple women ask me what I think about faking orgasms. I do have an opinion on the topic. I don't think it's such a hot idea.

Faking, in most cases, is a real cop-out. You don't have to work at the real thing—you can just pretend that you did. Better to lovingly tell your husband, "I'm sorry I couldn't orgasm, but you still satisfy me," than to fake.

Now, I do think there is a difference between *faking* and moaning or sighing during sex even when you don't feel like it. Making sounds and acting like you're enjoying sex more than you really are serves a purpose. Your body often tricks you, and before you know it, you really *are* turned on, and the moans and groans are the real thing.

One friend told me, "I often pretend like we're doing it for the first time. I'll make sounds and act like I'm really enjoying it and focus on that, and then usually I begin to feel that way, too."

Think of it this way: It's kind of like acting excited when your husband shares his morning's golfing experience with you, or his latest project at work. Face it—it doesn't excite you. Acting like it does is nicer than saying that you couldn't care less. And when you listen to him in this way, sometimes you do get excited about what interests him.

Faking an orgasm, however, is more like lying. Saying something happened when it really didn't. And when it becomes a habit, faking in bed is a deception your marriage doesn't need. Imagine how your husband would feel if, after months, even years, of thinking he was bringing you intense pleasure, he realized you'd been faking. He's not going to trust you—especially during sex.

You'll be like the boy who cried, "Wolf!" Even a real orgasm will leave your husband wondering, *Is it all a hoax?* You don't want your sex life to be built on a lie.

Trust certainly works the other way too. Because orgasms are such a mental and emotional thing, it can be very hard to reach this sexual plateau if you have trouble trusting your husband. Ask God to help you let down your guard and make yourself vulnerable. Hand your fears over to Him—let them go.

Pray that your bedroom (or wherever you have sex) will be an environment where you feel safe in an emotional sense, a place where you feel comfortable baring not just your body, but the deepest parts of your soul.

This will not happen overnight. Trust must be built over a period of time. But you can take small steps each day. Hopefully, as you put into practice the marriage-building tips you've read in this book and spend lots of time in prayer, your sexual encounters with your husband will be a place where freedom reigns. Freedom to give and receive—to give of yourself and to receive all that your husband has to offer you.

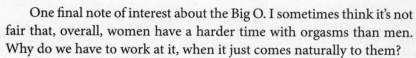

One final note of interest about the Big O. I sometimes think it's not fair that, overall, women have a harder time with orgasms than men. Why do we have to work at it, when it just comes naturally to them?

And then I remember something: ours are better. Dr. Leman comments,

> Many women are surprised when I tell them that a large percentage of men are jealous of their orgasms…From a guy's perspective, it looks like the world is exploding.

Your husband's orgasm will last for just a few seconds, while yours can be multiple. It keeps going and going and going. There are two basic forms multiple orgasms can take: the continuous orgasm that comes in wave after wave after wave and the kind that falls into a wave/rest/wave/rest/wave pattern. Either one is perfectly lovely.

One of my close friends is my hero—the Orgasm Queen. She's been married for almost 20 years and has all kinds of helpful, godly advice. When I asked her to describe the perfect sexual experience, she shared some juicy details and then added something she knows isn't possible but she thinks would be really cool.

"I'd love it if my husband could have as many orgasms as me," she said. "I generally have five to eight. No kidding. Praise God!"

Keep working on those orgasms. With time, effort, and prayer, you'll get to where you want to be. And when the day comes that you experience this fabulous phenomenon my friend is talking about, you and your hubby will both be shouting, "Hallelujah!"

Chapter 9

The Admiration Effect

Before you got married, did you have a checklist of standards to be met in a potential mate? What kinds of qualities made your list? A believer in Christ? Honors his parents? Loves kids? Tall, dark, and handsome? Smart? Romantic?

Checklists are a great thing to have, but every now and again, we have to watch our motives behind the lists. We get caught up in all the things *we* want, and that God-honoring checklist starts to take a selfish twist.

We find ourselves asking, "Will this guy make me happy and keep me satisfied for the rest of my life? If I marry this guy, will I ever again lack any good thing I need? Is he equipped to keep me contented, even if I tend to be somewhat high-maintenance? Is he an unselfish sort of chap, one who will always put my needs above his own? Is he going to age gracefully, mature in a timely fashion, and make me proud to be his wife?"

Are you starting to see the problem here? We become so focused on *ourselves* that we totally forget—or never even acknowledge in the first place—that marriage is all about giving and serving another. A truth that many young brides find hard to stomach.

"Say what? Giving and serving? Unselfishness and sacrifice? Well, that's no fun!" Or worse yet, "No man is going to run *my* life!"

The good news? Believe it or not, giving and serving ultimately bring greater happiness than selfishly grabbing, taking, and demanding your own way. Really. Ask someone who has tried it both ways, like yours truly.

He Can Do No Right

I've noticed a disturbing pattern in my marriage. When Gabe and I were dating, I could have made a list a mile long of all the things I loved about him. I actually did a time or two—"50 Reasons Why I'll Always and Forever Love Only You" or something equally corny.

But the longer we're married, the shorter that list becomes. And a new list has taken its place: "501 Things About You That Annoy/Irritate/Bother/Anger Me."

Nothing escapes my notice. The morning breath. The snoring. The failure to cut his toenails on a timely basis. The yard that needs to be mowed…and weeded…and fertilized. The prickly facial hair. The gas-passing. Oh, I could go on forever. According to Gabe, I probably do.

Whatever happened to the adoration and praise? Pointing out his best qualities and letting him know how lucky I am to have married him?

Why do I feel the need to inject a subtle (or not so subtle) negative jab into our conversations at every turn?

"Do you have to chew your food so loudly?"

"You haven't bought me flowers in quite a while."

"You're already done working for the day? You do know it's only four o'clock, right?"

"When do you think you might be able to turn your computer off and squeeze in some quality time with your family?"

What about thanking him for providing for our family so I can stay home? Or praising him for playing Prince Charming to our daughters' Cinderella? Or admiring his gorgeous eyes, strong hands, and broad shoulders?

What about thanking him for taking out the trash and carrying in the groceries? Or praising him for his creative talents and innovative ideas? Or thanking him for his commitment to fidelity and guarding his eyes and heart from impurity?

What about noticing the fact that kids and old ladies positively adore him? Or that his Web-design talents are in the highest demand? Or that I think he's more handsome now than the day we met?

What about all of that?

You don't know my husband, you're thinking. *He's not the same person he was when we were dating. He's just let himself go to pot.*

Bag the Nag

Honey, you might want to look in a mirror. I know I need to! And not just at my physical appearance. We need to find a mirror that reflects our inner self—our thoughts, our attitudes.

If we're honest, we'll admit he's not the only one who has changed. Look at yourself for a moment through your husband's eyes. If he were making a gripe list about *you,* what things would be on it?

Gabe's might include short temper, selfish with her time, often dresses like a slob, overly critical, impatient, doesn't like to be proved wrong, hard to please, too task-oriented, always nagging and never satisfied...

I'm not sure where we women have gotten the idea that nagging is our right. Or even that it works. It isn't. It doesn't. We want our husbands to change, so we start criticizing and nitpicking. While these tactics might make hubby try harder for a short period of time, eventually he'll give up.

Our husbands really do live for our approval. We know this, so we manipulate and abuse them to get what we want. But what do we *really* want? We want our men to stand up like men, but we fail to treat them like men.

"Bow down to me!" we might as well demand.

"Stand up for yourself!" we harp.

Bow down! Stand up! Which is it?

And if I'm not busy complaining about *him,* I'm usually moaning or whining about this, that, and the other thing. I can find something wrong with just about anything. I can spot holes in a silver lining from a mile away. Sometimes I act like my life is just one big bother. I'm only happy when I'm off doing my own thing.

In contrast, "Men live to make their women happy," Dr. Laura says. "The cruelest thing a wife can do to a husband is to never be happy. And don't forget, being happy is more an attitude than a reality."

Now I realize why Gabe has asked me numerous times, "Are you happy? You don't seem happy."

This was such a huge eye-opener for me. I need to make a conscious effort to be happy. Joyful. Optimistic. What good is it to go through life dwelling on the tiny little hindrances and forget about the millions of blessings I have? Going through life with a stinky attitude is a waste of precious, God-given time.

Find the Good

Now back to your husband, who you think has "gone to pot." You may not see it right away, but I'm willing to bet he actually still possesses many of those same qualities that attracted you to him in the first place. You probably just aren't paying attention anymore.

Why not tell him some of the things you love about him? After all, as the proverb says, "Pleasant words are a honeycomb, sweet to the soul and healing to the bones."

Of course, it does no good to say one thing and do another. So, don't shower him with empty words of praise and then ignore him or treat him like dirt or refuse sex or purposely do things you know will annoy him. Your walk will have to back up your talk.

We take so many things for granted. Recognize the good in your husband and verbally acknowledge it. I try to always thank Gabe for mowing the lawn, taking out the trash, raking leaves, shoveling snow, grilling steaks, earning money, playing with our girls, and so on. Don't take him for granted!

Thank your husband for being funny. Growing spiritually. Managing your money. Bringing in money. Being smart. Being attractive. His physical features. Being a good daddy. Working hard. Helping others. Honoring his parents.

What kinds of things can you tell *your* husband that will help him to know you appreciate him?

What we choose to focus on inevitably takes a prominent place in our minds. The state of our marriage is often a reflection of how we choose to think about it—not how things actually are. Dwelling on positives and downplaying the negatives can make a so-so marriage so much better.

Part of the reason we think our spouses are doing such a lousy job is because we have tuned out everything but the negative about them. We've programmed our eyes, ears, and brain to pick up only those signals that carry hints—whether real or imagined—of negativity. We skip right over any good thing our husbands do or positive step they take. It's all negative, all the time.

James warns us that "a word out of your mouth may seem of no account, but it can accomplish nearly anything—or destroy it!"*

What would happen if we adjusted our dials and tuned in to a station broadcasting only our husbands' positive traits and actions? And for 48 hours, what if we sat by our radio and took meticulous notes? And then shared our discoveries—what we *noticed*—with our husbands?

Stop nagging your husband for an entire day. If it doesn't matter, let it go. Fight the urge to open your mouth. Bite your tongue every time you get the urge to say something critical or sarcastic. A whole day. Then extend it another day. And another. And replace your usual rude and biting remarks with kind and positive ones. Don't just leave big, empty, silent gaps.

We do a fine job of keeping mental lists of wrongs and offenses. What about trying a pen-and-paper list of happy-hubby thoughts—his good deeds and positive characteristics?

I tried this recently—and wow! Funny how I didn't notice the annoying things as much while taking notes only on the good ones.

Accept your husband for who he is. Quit trying so hard to make him something he's not. Show him that you love him. That you *need* him. "An anxious heart weighs a man down, but a kind word cheers him up," it says in the book of Proverbs.

Make him feel that you value his opinion, that you think he's

---

* James 3:5 MSG.

intelligent. Let him share his feelings without consequence. Feelings are not *wrong*; they're subjective.

Don't talk to him with ulterior motives. Don't make him pass a test—answer a certain way—or be damned. Don't demand (or even imply) that he must always agree with everything you say. Or that he dare not criticize a word or challenge you in any way.

"So let's agree to use all our energy in getting along with each other," Paul says in Romans 14 in *The Message* paraphrase. "Help others with encouraging words; don't drag them down by finding fault."

Let your husband know you believe in him. He just might become the husband you've always dreamed he would be. It's definitely working for me in my marriage.

Getting Physical

There are two things women say to their husbands that trouble me: 1) I'm not pleased with your physical appearance, and 2) someone else's physical appearance pleases me greatly.

"Both dropping hints about desired physical changes and showing undue admiration of someone other than your mate will break down your spouse's sense of being accepted," says Dr. Gardner.

What your husband looks like is not the point. There is never a right time to criticize your husband's body—especially those traits he can't change. I'm not saying you can't gently encourage him to live a healthy lifestyle, but watch yourself. You're probably better off praying that *God* will convict him to change his eating and exercise habits than to hint-drop.

Unfortunately, more often than not, we'd like our husbands to change (lose weight, shave facial hair, get a tan) for selfish reasons. We think those changes will make us happier and reflect better on us, their wives.

Yes, society is admittedly kinder to men when it comes to their appearance. We realize this. However, this does *not* mean that men are immune to the pain that careless (or even rude) comments about their bodies can cause.

If your husband feels fat, ugly, or physically inadequate because of cruel remarks you have made, you have seriously dishonored him. No matter what your husband's physical appearance is, you should be the one person who always makes him feel completely loved and accepted.

And as for complimenting other guys on how they look, I'm going to jump up on another soapbox here. I don't think it's cool when women rant and rave about actors or athletes they think are "sooo hot." I can't remember the last time I said that of a man other than my husband, and it's not because I'm blind. I have purposefully chosen not to voice my opinion of attractive men. And I've purposefully chosen not to dwell on the attractive appearance of other guys, even in my mind.

I think of it this way: Do I really want my husband watching a movie with me and saying, "Wow, so-and-so is hot!" and then thinking about her for the rest of the day and night? No, I really don't.

Getting Spiritual

Another big problem I've seen—in my own marriage as well—is wives wanting their husbands to be more "spiritual." A godly man is an attractive man.

Let me give it to you straight, sister: If you are ignoring your husband's needs and desires (particularly for sex), he is going to deeply resent you for pushing God and the Bible on him. Not to mention the fact that by ignoring his needs, you are explicitly disobeying one of the Bible's commands yourself.

The merits of an intimate relationship with the Lord can only be discovered by your husband on his own (or what he *thinks* is on his own but is actually God answering your faithful, silent prayers on his behalf).

Into Bed and into Church

I have a friend whose husband wasn't the slightest bit interested in anything spiritual. In fact, he was pretty hostile toward anything related to God.

Then Kate read a book that changed her marriage. She began to initiate sex with Charlie and to be a more willing participant in bed. What started as determination in her mind soon melted into real feelings— she wanted Charlie physically and emotionally.

The changes in Charlie came slowly but surely. A little smoother, a little kinder, a little more open to going to church. And Kate knows exactly why.

Don't tell your husband, "I'd feel so much closer to you if you'd read your Bible and initiate prayer time with me." Yeah, I've done this.

What you might try instead is willingly, happily giving your husband all the sex he needs and wants and *then* casually mentioning (after much prayer for wisdom) that you'd love it if the two of you could extend your newfound physical and emotional intimacy into a spiritual arena as well.

Tell Him He's Your (Hot) Hero

I asked women to share with me some positive things about their hubbies when it comes to making love. Keep in mind that these are women who struggle with their sex lives, who don't always understand their husbands, who oftentimes find their mates annoying. But they still found things to praise their husbands for—in a specific way. Hopefully, they'll take it one step further and share it with their husbands themselves.

> "He's unselfish about it. He almost always precedes sex with just being a good husband that day. He knows it's not as enjoyable for me if he's been preoccupied all day."

> "He's really good about pleasuring me before. I had heard guys really like to jump into it, but he doesn't. That means a lot to me."

> "He is great in bed, very unselfish 98 percent of the time. The other 2 percent, he just can't help himself."

> "He prolongs his orgasm so I can try to have one."

> "My husband is very understanding and patient when it comes to what I want or don't want from our sex life and is willing to do just about anything to improve it."

> "He's fun in bed. He enjoys it and makes me feel alluring and feminine, stretch marks and all."

> "He treats me with respect and has always been careful to be 'gentle' during sex."

Even if words of affirmation aren't your husband's primary "love language," *everybody* warms to a genuine compliment. One thing we can do to help us make big strides toward a great sex life is to praise our husbands for their prowess in the bedroom. Here are some ideas to rev your hubby's motor:

- "You look really hot tonight."
- "You know exactly where to touch me, don't you?"
- "How did you get so good at lovemaking?"
- "Do you have any idea how badly I want you tonight?"
- "You've got to have the hottest body on the planet."
- "You are so strong."
- "I love the way your muscles ripple when we're making love."
- "You touch my _____ perfectly."

If you want more ideas, take your cue from the heroine in the Song of Songs. She's constantly talking up her darling with words like, "How handsome you are, my lover! Oh, how charming! And our bed is verdant." (I wouldn't necessarily use the word *verdant* unless your husband is a human dictionary—or an avid gardener.)

Tell him in so many words that he's your hero. Be creative. Don't worry about sounding stupid. I've said some pretty dumb things in my day, and Gabe has eaten them right up!

Make Your Praise Public

There are some definite do's and don'ts about how you treat your husband when you're around other people. Stay away from gripe sessions with girlfriends. Either find new friends, or you be the one to start praising your husband when everyone else is cutting theirs down.

One thing you can do to affirm your husband is to show him physical affection in public. You don't need to kiss, grope, fondle, and paw each other in plain view of everyone and his brother—eww! But let your body language communicate to those around you that you find this guy attractive and desirable. Don't be so obvious that you have people shouting, "Get a room!" but show enough tenderness that those people subconsciously think, "They'll be getting it on later, I bet."

Show him verbal affection as well. Praise him out loud in front of others. Let him know he's worth bragging about to your family and friends.

While you're at it, lose the sarcasm. Avoid it like the plague, no matter how funny it seems at the time. Sarcasm may seem like solid proof we're witty, intelligent, and quick on our feet, but it is often cruel. Funny or no, tucked away inside three-fourths of all sarcastic remarks is some form of bitterness, anger, or jealousy. There's always an element of truth to it, which makes it painful.

In chapter 3 of his first letter in the Bible, Peter exhorts his readers to be kind and loving to each other. "No sharp-tongued sarcasm," reads *The Message*. "Instead, bless—that's your job, to bless. You'll be a blessing and also get a blessing."

I find myself drawn to women who talk about their husbands in a positive light. Not the gushy type who go on and on about their darling beloveds; not the fakey type who don't really like their husbands but are just trying to impress everyone. I'm talking about the genuine women who, when talking about their husbands, have a big smile on their faces. The ones who give their mates the benefit of the doubt, never drag their name through the mud, never share things that would embarrass their husbands if they knew they were being shared.

I want to be one of these women.

LENDING HUBBY A HAND

Chapter 10

Don't Leave Him Guessing

My friend Amanda was giddy with excitement. She had replayed the scenario over and over in her mind, and it was finally time to live it! It was her wedding night. The hour drive to the hotel was over.

Still clad in her gorgeous gown, tiara, and high heels, Amanda couldn't wait to get up to the room. She smiled as she envisioned her romantic new husband carrying her over the threshold, placing her gently on the bed, and sexily removing her from her gown. The passion that ensued would be electrifying.

Or not. Turns out Nathan couldn't find his wallet. "Go on up to the room and get ready," he told Amanda. "It's got to be here in the truck somewhere." (It was in his tux pants pocket back at the church.)

Get ready? Amanda thought. *I* am *ready!* Things were not going as planned. She went up to the room, had a little cry, fixed her makeup, sprayed on some perfume, lay on the bed trying to look sexy, and waited. And waited.

No Nathan. More waiting. And waiting.

Finally, she went down to the truck where he was tearing it apart looking for his wallet. She went back upstairs, climbed out of her dress, and dug into the food she had missed out on during the reception.

The next morning involved a car trip back to his parents to retrieve the missing wallet followed by an eight-hour trip to their honeymoon destination. After listening to Nathan complain about having to drag her "dumb dress" around with them, Amanda snapped back that her ideal wedding night had involved him taking her passionately *out* of that "dumb dress." Of course he had no idea.

Maybe the rest of the honeymoon would go more smoothly, Amanda hoped. They would spend most of their time in their room, leaving only to go sightseeing or shopping. They'd hold hands as they strolled leisurely along. They'd eat romantic dinners at nice restaurants, sitting on the same side of the booth like lovers do.

Or not. Amanda had unknowingly scheduled their wedding date smack dab in the middle of March Madness. All Nathan wanted to do was watch college basketball on TV. He hated shopping, didn't want to miss any games, and didn't like the idea of public displays of affection. They couldn't agree on eating places, and he sat *across* from Amanda, much to her chagrin.

Their honeymoon concluded with Amanda in tears, bawling, "You don't love me! You don't love me!" while Nathan wrung his hands, thinking, *What in the world have I gotten myself into?*

How's a Guy to Know?

I don't know about you, but I pretty much expect my husband to be clued in to my needs and desires. This isn't our honeymoon anymore. We *have* been married for almost eight years now. After all that time, how could he not know what I'm thinking? He has no excuse.

We're not asking for much from our husbands really. We just want them to read our minds. When something's bothering us, and they ask what's wrong, we shoot them a glare that could kill and spew the words, "How could you not *know?*"

Well, that's an easy one. He doesn't know because men aren't mind-readers. But it's not their fault. They're trying.

I talk extensively about our unrealistic expectations for marriage in my book *From Blushing Bride to Wedded Wife*. In this chapter, I'm going to focus on our unrealistic expectations for *sex*.

It's not so much that we expect *too much* from our husbands in the bedroom. It's just that we don't let them know what those expectations are!

Believe me, your husband wants to know how to turn you on! Genuinely turning you on—absolutely no faking—is one of his greatest pleasures in life. But since he can't read your mind, he has to resort to figuring out *on his own* what makes you go, floats your boat, flips your skirt.

Mission: impossible.

Too bad he's not a woman. And even if he was, he wouldn't know what turns *you* on in particular. No two women are alike—especially in bed. One woman wants her such-and-such caressed during lovemaking, and the next woman would rather eat worms than be touched there. How's a guy to know?

And then there's the fact that what turns you on one night fails miserably the next. It's a woman's prerogative to change her mind, right?

Do our poor husbands have a prayer?

What We Don't Like

Heather knows what I'm talking about. "I'm turned off when Curt tries to turn me on the same way every time," she told me.

"Have you talked to him about this?" I wanted to know.

"Yes," she says. "I tell him that the same stuff doesn't always work and we have a good laugh. Then he'll try other things until he finds something that he thinks works every time. And we'll talk again…"

Katherine loves it when her husband touches her between the legs, while "fondling between the legs" is the one thing that bothers Leslie most.

"I haven't told him it bothers me, though," Leslie says, "because I want to grow in this area for his sake."

Jenna gets turned on when she and Drew "take a nice hot shower together." Whenever Gabe and I attempt a simultaneous shower, I end up hyperventilating.

Holly loves it when Mike "talks dirty" to her, while Erin says, "When he tries to talk dirty, I end up sounding like a piece of meat. It's an instant turn-off."

Hannah doesn't like it when her husband talks *at all* during sex.

While some women may enjoy the feel of their husband's tongue in their ear, Jada doesn't like too much of it. "A little goes a long way there," she says.

Tammy's not a fan of what she calls "Wham-Bam-Thank-You-Ma'am" sex, where it all happens really quick and when her husband's done, that's the end of it.

Marin, on the other hand, thinks quickies are sexy, "especially in the afternoon."

There *are* a few things most of us women agree just don't do it for us.

Bad breath, for one. Stacey says that she and Jeff "just try to avoid breathing in each other's face when either of us complains, but often I don't say anything so as not to interrupt things."

Body odor is another one. Elise says that if Devin "comes home from work smelling funky I prefer him to take a shower, or I suggest we take a bath together."

"I hate long toenails!" Liz says. "Thankfully, Brian is usually good about keeping his nails neat and trim."

Katherine isn't all that thrilled when Kevin passes gas in bed, but when she talks to him about it, he just laughs. "He really can't help it," she says with a gracious smile.

Tell Him Gently

A wife has to be careful when telling her husband, "I don't like that." Or else hurt feelings and damaged egos result.

You have to know your husband well and anticipate how he might react before you start blurting things out. Choose your words carefully. Prefacing them with some positives is the way to go.

Using "I" statements instead of "you" statements is a good start. For example, instead of "You try to go so fast, you ruin the whole experience for me!" try, "Honey, all I need is some slow, tender loving, and then I'll be rarin' to go!"

Avoid blanket statements and words like "never" and "always."

"You *never* kiss me how I want to be kissed!" or "Why do you *always* start groping me before I'm ready?"

Sometimes nonverbal communication works, and sometimes it doesn't. Erin doesn't like her husband talking dirty to her, and while she's never verbally stated that fact to him, she says, "I give him a certain look that gets the message across."

And what is hubby's response? "He acts a little offended when I do that," she says.

Maybe in Erin's case, verbal communication would be better. She could tell her husband kindly how it makes her feel when he talks dirty. She could let him know how much she loves him and offer suggestions for words he could use that would still be sexy to him but not offensive to her.

Another option is for Erin to pray about this and ask God if this is an area she needs to grow in. When our husbands ask us to do things that make us uncomfortable, I think it's good to spend time in prayer and honestly ask God, "Does this make me uncomfortable because it's something that's not right for us as a couple? Or is it something I need to work at, so that I feel more comfortable with this thing that means so much to my husband?"

God will answer your heartfelt request.

When Jamie told Daniel that she didn't like it when he kissed her forcefully, his feelings were hurt. Perhaps Jamie could have started out by saying, "Daniel, I love it when you kiss me. I feel so close to you, and it turns me on. Sometimes, it hurts me a little when you kiss me really hard. Could we have a little signal that I could give you anytime the kissing gets too rough?"

It Worked for Me

Here are some success stories:

"I didn't like it when he would try to kiss me after giving me oral sex," Jenna admits, "or when he tried to stimulate me by touching my anus." She gently explained her feelings to her husband.

His response? "He was very understanding and now he doesn't do either of those things."

"He's not as gentle as I need him to be when we've gone a long time without having sex," Carly says.

After sharing her feelings with her husband honestly but tactfully, "he slows down and tries not to hurt me," she says.

Lissa had an interesting complaint. "Sometimes he's just too polite," she says of her husband, wishing he'd rough things up a bit. When she tells him how she feels, her manners man replies, "I'm sorry, sweetie."

Sometimes the solution isn't telling your husband that he's irritating you but just doing your best not to let it bother you.

"My husband has this awful noise he makes when he's really into making me excited," Molly says. "I can't really describe it. It's a kind of smacking noise with his lips. It sounds like he's chewing food or something and really turns me off."

Has Molly shared her irritation with her husband? "Yes," she says, "and he's tried to stop, but he does it without thinking and it hurts him when I make a comment about it."

So, what is Molly to do?

"I've decided to stop being so sensitive to it," she says. "In the past, I would just lie there waiting for him to do it. Now, I try to focus on something else, or just tell myself he's only doing it because I'm really turning him on. It's part of his whole language of love."

A Man's Perspective

As a marriage psychologist, Dr. Kevin Leman has a distinct advantage over most husbands. In *Sheet Music,* he tells a story of a man named Jim who listened for his wife's audible clues in bed. All it took was a single moan from her, and he'd use whatever trick he was doing at the time the next 50 times they made love.

Dr. Leman kindly explained to Jim that while men often treat sex like a football playbook—knowing exactly what move will come next—women like more variety, less routine. "Your job is to figure out which way the wind is blowing on that particular day," he told Jim.

This is a big job for our husbands, girls. We need to help them out.

We women are suckers for "presentation." We like things to look just right. And men just don't get this. We wives have got to find ways—some subtle, some not so much—to hint at what we'd like. Your husband might not realize that showering and donning some new silk boxers will nearly always trump the ol' run-up-the-stairs-and-flop-on-the-bed-in-all-your-nude-and-sweaty-splendor tactic.

So, men aren't naturally intuitive. We've picked up on that. The question is what are we going to do about it? Sit around moping about the fact that they don't understand us? Or tell them what we want?

"If you want to frustrate a man," Dr. Leman says, "tell him nothing. Make him keep throwing darts into the dark, hoping he gets lucky."

That's not what we want.

I think we're doing our husbands a great disservice by leaving them in the dark. Besides, it's often nothing more than a cop-out. If I don't tell him what I want, he won't give it to me, and then I'm free to keep my distance and be ticked at his insensitivity, right?

Welcome to Hollywood

Another huge disservice we can do our mates is to compare (subconsciously or otherwise) our sex lives to those of others. I'm thinking of people on television or the silver screen in particular. Have you ever resented your husband for not being as romantic and sexy as a character in a movie?

If you entered marriage thinking sex would be fabulous and amazing all the time and have been sorely disappointed, you can blame it (at least in part) on the media to which you've been exposed—movies, TV, romance novels, magazines. The media presents things in a purposeful and calculated way, fully intending to feed us lie after lie. And sadly, we eat those lies up—and come back for more.

For couples in movies and on TV, writes Karen Linamen,

> Lovemaking is always steamy and never troubled.
> Sex is always hot and always available. Orgasms fly fast

and furious. Women have perfect bodies, and men are perfect lovers.

In *Blushing Bride*, I ask my readers to visualize a typical scene involving a dating couple in the movies. After dinner, drinks, and a slow walk under the stars, said couple heads to her place—namely her bedroom—where things start to get steamy.

Fast-forward to a frame I call "The Delightful Morning After." You know, the rollover in bed, pat the pillow dreamily. He's gone, but there's a rose, a note, the sun streaming in the window. The clean white sheets, tousled hair, the contented sigh and goofy smile.

No mention of diaphragms or condoms, smelly underwear or bad breath, leg cramps or a mess of any sort. She wakes up naked, beautiful, and exhilarated, on a cloud of pure loveliness, without so much as a hint of a stain on the sheets or a streak of dried semen down her leg.

When you wake up on the morning after your honeymoon, this scene is what you have naturally come to expect, having played it over and over in your mind. Instead, your crotch is throbbing, your hair is flattened against your head in a most unflattering way, and you can smell your husband's breath—and body—a mile away. There's no note or rose, just your hunk of man sprawled across the bed beside you, snoring with his mouth wide open.

You get up to pee and find yourself dripping all the way to the bathroom. When you look in the mirror, you discover a huge zit developing on your nose. And then you remember the worst of it—you couldn't orgasm and your husband got really frustrated. You were so tight and tense that sex felt no less painful than how you've always imagined childbirth without an epidural.

And in the weeks and months that follow, you never once have that dreamy "Movie Girl" experience. Just a nasty urinary tract infection. How did things go so excruciatingly wrong? Maybe you married the wrong guy!

"We aren't supposed to have to work at sex," Karen Linamen says. "It's just supposed to be there, fully bloomed and perfect, like some sort of inalienable right implied, although not spelled out, in our Constitution."

Even if we know in our heads that Movie Girl sex is unrealistic, we still long for it in our hearts. And while we like to think of ourselves as free thinkers, not easily swayed by what we see and read, we're deceiving ourselves. We *are* influenced by what we see and read, and nowhere does this fact manifest itself more clearly than when it comes to sex. We really, truly expect sex to be like it is in the movies.

"How *does* Flick Chick do it?" we want to know. The good news is that she doesn't. She's not real. None of it is real. It's a movie. People are airbrushed. Blemishes are edited. Bad breath doesn't exist. There is no mess. It's effortless. There are no disappointments to deal with, complex

Sex and Burgers

Picture a TV commercial advertising a new bacon cheese-burger. The hamburger is huge and luscious, the tomatoes ripe and juicy, the lettuce crisp and fresh, dripping with ice water, the bun is full and fluffy, the cheese melted and gooey, there are at least four strips of thick, meaty bacon, and the guy in the commercial can barely fit the thing in his mouth.

Fast-forward to the next day when you actually go to this fast food joint and order the aforementioned burger. The meat is measly, the tomatoes are hard and green around the edges, the lettuce is brown and wilted, the bun is smashed, the cheese is cold, and you're lucky to get two tiny strips of bacon! What happened?

What you see on TV is not always what you get. Not with bacon cheeseburgers, and definitely not with sex. Juicy-looking cheeseburgers sell, and so does juicy-looking sex. Real life just doesn't cut it in the media market.

We'd do well to go on a fast from TV, movies, and romantic novels for a while. Concentrate on our own lives, our own husbands, our own bedrooms. Make our real lives as good as they can be. (And they can be really good.)

And quit expecting our husbands to transport us to some fantasy world they don't even know exists.

issues that come up, differences of opinion to navigate through, or problems to tackle.

Repeat after me. *It. Is. Not. Real.*

Things We Like

When I asked women to share some happy thoughts about hubby in the bedroom, they had lots to tell. The key is to share those thoughts with your husband. Let him know he has succeeded at his goal to please you. Oftentimes, what pleases us most are things that don't come naturally to a man—a man who doesn't need the things you need. And when your desires change, kindly voice that as well.

I love it when my husband…

- spends time kissing and caressing and talking to me before the act of sex.
- tells me I'm pretty.
- just seems to love my body…by looking at me, touching me, things like that.
- rubs my back.
- acts assertive and tells me exactly what he wants.
- nibbles my neck.
- gives me oral sex.
- massages me—it helps me relax and focus on sex.
- initiates sex, takes charge, is on top.
- leaves my panties on and works around them.
- squeezes my rear end and kisses my breasts.
- prolongs his release to try and give me a chance to orgasm.
- spends time helping me to get ready to make love by giving me oral stimulation.
- wants me and I can tell.
- rubs up against me, talks to me, kisses me.
- licks and touches me.
- lights candles and uses massage oils.

Solomon's wife was great at telling him what she enjoyed and wanted from him: "Kiss me—full on the mouth!…Take me away with you! Let's run off together!"*

Just because you're married doesn't mean you have the right to the fulfillment of every sexual fantasy and desire. But it certainly doesn't hurt to *ask*. Write down a play-by-play commentary for your husband—how you would like your next sexual encounter to go. Your idea of a perfect sexual experience. And remember to include some things you'll do for *him*—it's not all about you.

The flip side of this is to ask your husband what *he* genuinely likes. Chances are, his desires are more physical and sexual, while yours are more cuddly and romantic. (But not always.) If we're going to be unselfish lovers, though, we have to give more than we take. Or at the very least, give *just as much* as we take.

The Wish List

In order for your love life to be fulfilling, you've got to know what you *both* want. As silly as it sounds, make a Wish List and suggest that your husband do the same. Write your lists separately and then come together and discuss them. Ask questions like, How often would you like to have sex? What sexual fantasy do you have? How much foreplay is ideal for you? What gets you in the mood?

Figure out which requests are doable and which ones are unreasonable. Ask each other, "Would you do this for me?" Stretch yourself, but be honest. Try using something like these general categories:

1. Forget it!
2. Possibly—if we compromise.
3. Pretty likely—with these changes.
4. Sure, why not? That sounds awesome!

Where and how can you do a little give and take so each person feels like some of his or her needs are being met? Compromise. Negotiate. If, when you discuss your Wish Lists, they appear to have nothing in common, hold a peace summit of sorts. You give a little on this point. He concedes on this one.

---

* Song of Songs 1:2,4 msg.

Be careful, though. Negotiating can turn into a negative thing. "I won't give you what *you* want until you give me what *I* want." Don't withhold sex as a punishment or means of getting something you want.

I watched a guy on *Oprah* once who paid his wife to have sex with him. He wanted sex. She didn't. He worked and got a paycheck. She didn't. She was actually getting the better end of the deal. She got money to go shopping—which is all she selfishly wanted anyway. But he missed out on what all men crave—a woman who truly wants him sexually. He sold out. Sex from a wife who doesn't want it will never ultimately satisfy. It won't be long before he's out looking for a new hooker.

I think it's okay to say, "I'll give you oral sex if you'll give me a 20-minute backrub afterward," but don't make a habit of giving just to get. Even though sex and marriage are theoretically give and take, you should be willing to give even when there's nothing to take.

We women are typically less adventurous in bed than our husbands, but this is not always the case. It may be that there are one or two (or more) desires or fantasies that you share candidly with your husband, and he shoots you an unbelieving look and says, "Not a chance."

You can't—and shouldn't—force your husband to do something that makes him uncomfortable (giving you oral sex, for example). Offer to negotiate. If he's not willing, don't push. Drop the matter for the time being. If it's really important to you, take it to God in prayer. Ask Him to either change your husband's heart or take away that particular desire.

Our job is to share our sexual desires, not pressure our husbands to fulfill them. Once they know how they can serve us best, we leave the decision to serve—or not—up to them.

You must verbalize how you feel. You cannot expect your husband to read your mind. Yes, it's romantic when he can. And that may come with time. One of these days, your wonderful husband might surprise you. Mine has. But until he does, telling him what you want is far better than being frustrated and disappointed when he just can't figure it out.

Chapter 11

The "Other" Kind of Sex

When I was in college, I had a couple Christian friends who engaged in oral sex with their boyfriends and thought it was morally acceptable. "We're still virgins," they argued. "We've never had real sex."

I wholeheartedly disagree. In my opinion, separating sexual activities into various categories is generally done to justify sex outside of marriage. As long as it's not vaginal intercourse, you haven't actually had sex. This way, if you want to be a "technical virgin," and still have oral sex, you can.

Sex is a whole. All of its "parts" are intertwined into a pleasurable and intimate experience reserved for a man and his wife. I never had oral sex before marriage, but I did indulge in snatches of the whole intimate experience of sex that should have been saved—in its entirety—for marriage.

Is (Married) Oral Sex Okay?

Once you've tied the knot, I believe that oral sex is perfectly acceptable, and I've never second-guessed my opinion.

So I was surprised to find that a few women I surveyed either weren't sure that it was permissible, or they felt very strongly that it's not.

When asked, "If you weren't too embarrassed, what would you ask a Christian marriage/sex counselor?" one woman said, "Is oral sex okay?"

"What things do you think are off-limits for a Christian couple when it comes to sex?" I wanted to know.

"Anything expressly forbidden in the Bible," one woman said, "and oral sex."

"Nothing really. Except oral sex," said another.

I respect these women, and they are absolutely entitled to their opinions. At the same time, I disagree that oral sex in marriage is wrong.*

It's true that oral sex has gotten a bad rap in the past. Some states still have laws against it on the books. I'm not sure how they enforce these laws, but that's beside the point.

The Bible doesn't specifically address oral sex, but let's take a look at some of the explicit lyrics in the Song of Songs: "His fruit is sweet to my taste"; "Let my lover come into his garden and taste its choice fruits"; and so on. Many Bible teachers believe these verses refer to using your mouth to stimulate your partner's genitals—oral sex, that is.

Even if these verses are referring to something else, the argument from God's silence is substantial. He forbids many things, but oral sex is not one of them.

Dr. Kevin Leman raises a good question. Why can you kiss someone on the lips but not somewhere else? What about the breasts, toes, or behind the knees? The inner thigh? The genitals? Where to draw the line?

Some women's main complaint about oral sex is that it's unclean. Too bad that argument doesn't hold water. A woman's mouth has way more germs than her husband's freshly washed penis. "If you're truly concerned

---

* If you haven't done so already, you really need to pick up a copy of Dr. Kevin Leman's *Sheet Music*. Chapter 7, "Oral Delights," is a great read, and I found it most helpful and enlightening. I'm going to draw on some key points from Dr. Leman to help me make my case for oral sex.

about hygiene," Dr. Leman comments, "forget mouth-to-mouth kissing and go straight to oral sex!"

He is careful to add that oral sex should never be forced, and if you

A Recipe for Pleasure

Tease with tiny licks for a few seconds. Then cover his entire penis with your mouth if possible. Come up for air when you need to. Take little breaks of light blowing, kissing, etc. Ask him what feels good, what he'd like. Moans? Licks? The underside of the penis is more sensitive to touch—take advantage of that. Use your hands and fingers for added stimulation and so your mouth and jaw don't get so tired.

Other ideas? Appeal to your husband's visual nature by looking up at him while you pleasure him. Give oral sex by candlelight. Tie your hair back, so he can see what you're doing. Eat Altoids or suck on a cough drop first—your husband will feel the tingly menthol. Or keep taking sips of hot tea. An extra warm tongue is a new and exciting sensation.

What about swallowing? Swallowing semen isn't harmful, but if it's distasteful to you, pull your mouth away before your husband climaxes. Ask him to warn you. He'll know it's coming. You'll probably be able to tell too.

Many women are surprised to find that after giving oral sex a chance, they begin to see it as a pleasure rather than a duty.

"When a woman shows her own enjoyment in pleasuring her husband," Dr. Leman says, "she's giving him an unusually intense gift. Nothing will excite your man more than to know that you're excited—particularly as you do something to arouse him."

Give yourself a little pep talk. Think of all the good that will come of giving your husband this gift. Act excited, even if you aren't, and the excitement you end up feeling might catch you by surprise.*

---

* Since this is a book for women, I won't go into how your husband can perform oral sex on you. Have hubby read *Sheet Music*, pages 117-119, if he's willing and interested. Dr. Leman's key points? Not wanting oral sex done to you is often a matter of self-consciousness—a psychological hurdle. Take a shower first. Ask your husband to kiss his way slowly down your body—not just head straight for your genitals. Have him use his fingers as well—nails trimmed and filed. Have him ask you what feels good—or just tell him. Above all, remind him to be *gentle*.

are never willing to do it, that's okay. But, in the event that your husband would really enjoy it, and you want to bless him with a special treat, try the recipe in the sidebar, courtesy of Dr. Leman.

The Survey Says...

I asked four good friends to share with me some of their personal thoughts on oral sex. These gals have been married anywhere from two months to 20 years. Some of their comments are enlightening.

"We never thought much about it until after our first child was born," Liz says, "and intercourse was off limits for a few weeks. I actually asked my husband if I could try it for him. He loved it. It was fun just bringing him pleasure. I do think, though, that intercourse is much more pleasing for both of us. My husband said that although it felt great and was fun, he would much rather we both receive the pleasure together."

"My husband doesn't want to do it to me," reports Daphne, "and I haven't done it completely to him. It's just not something we find that desirable. I definitely think oral sex is acceptable in marriage, though. I'd say anything goes, unless it's something one of you doesn't feel comfortable with (but then perhaps you should learn to be comfortable with it—I'm not sure). I think husbands should be sensitive, but wives should be more willing. It's still a struggle for me that my body is not completely my own anymore, but I believe it's a sin to deny my husband pleasures that marriage should bring."

"I think Christian women should be informed on how to give their spouse oral sex," Lynn remarks. "How can a woman not like doing something her husband would love? And let's face it—I think most men love the idea of their wife doing that. Women need to know where to touch, how to move their mouth and tongue."

"I believe the Lord wants us to enjoy our spouses sexually as long as we are comfortable," Holly says. "Oral sex is wonderful as long as you are comfortable with it and enjoy it. We have to be understanding if our spouse doesn't like it. It takes a while to be comfortable doing sexual stuff that seems weird, but if both of you like it—and most importantly, if it honors God—then it will enhance your love for each other."

Taste and Comfort

As Lynn so bluntly put it, "How can a woman not like doing something her husband would love?" Though there are definitely selfish reasons for not liking oral sex, even with a good attitude, the act might still be distasteful to you. The smell and taste might seem unpleasant, or discomfort might discourage you from enjoying oral sex. Here are some tips that might help.

To improve his smell: Personally scrub his genital area with a yummy-smelling soap. Be sure to wash in all his cracks and crevices (in front and behind) and rinse well. Let him air out a while, and remove any stray pubic hairs that got rubbed off while you were scrubbing.

To improve the taste (also helps with the smell): Use whipped cream, a fruit-flavored lubricant, chocolate syrup, or something that tastes especially good to you. Squirt, rub, or spray some on and lick it off. Do it again. Kiss it off. And again. Suck it off. Make it yummy rather than yucky. (You can also try Altoids or hot tea—see the sidebar earlier.)

To improve the comfort factor: If you find yourself getting cramps in your arms, neck, and back while performing oral sex on your husband, try some new positions. You can even vary your position every few minutes. Have him sit on the edge of the bed or on a chair. Try having him stand up while you kneel. Or he can lie down but rub your neck and massage your shoulders while you work. Or play with your hair, if that's something you enjoy. Maybe the promise of a massage when you're done will be enough.

"I finally found a way to give my husband oral sex without getting nasty cramps in my neck and shoulders," Ellen says. "He sits back on the couch (with a towel underneath him—our couches are new!), and I kneel in front of him. He massages my head and neck while I do it, and it feels great to both of us. The massage relaxes me and helps me enjoy what I'm doing."

What about swallowing? I'll let you make your own call, but if I had to guess, I'd say an overwhelming majority of women couldn't make themselves do it. The taste and sensation are hard to stomach for most of us.

All Things Taboo

Are there certain things you just shouldn't do in bed—even after you're married? Are there sexual practices God prohibits? Are there topics on which He's silent but that just aren't right for a Christian couple?

When I asked women to share with me things they thought were off limits, the answers were varied. Most I agreed with; some I did not.

I have my own opinions, which I've tried to base on God's Word. When God tells us how we should or should not act, He's not just offering suggestions. He means business. But when He doesn't mention specifics, we have to make a decision on our own as a couple.

Many women I surveyed expressed their convictions that anal sex isn't something a married Christian couple should be doing. I agree. My personal opinion (and you're free to have yours) is that anal sex is unsafe and unhealthy. I believe that a woman's anus was simply not designed by her Creator to sustain intercourse.

With oral sex, your mouth is not harmed. With anal sex, there is the potential of tears and lesions in the rectal tissue. And if bacteria from the anus are introduced into the vagina, infection can occur.

No, the Bible does not say you can't do it. So, based on what information you do have, you'll have to make that judgment as a couple.

What about stimulating each other to orgasm without having intercourse—a "hand job," as it's commonly called? I personally don't see a problem with doing that for your husband occasionally, especially during your period or after you've just had a baby. But I don't think it should take the place of having intercourse regularly. It's just not as intimate and special as sex is. Again, you'll have to make the call as a couple.

Dr. Leman has a good way of putting it:

> The way you look at sex is the way *you* look at sex—but that doesn't make it the right way, or the only way to look at sex. I'm not saying there aren't any moral absolutes; I certainly believe there are. But I am saying that what we feel about sex within the context of marriage can be a very individual thing.

What other things did my survey-takers feel should be left out of your sexual repertoire?

"Swinging," one woman said. "Third parties," said another. "Involving other people." "Threesomes." "Trading partners."

Whatever you want to call it, this one's a given. God created sex to be between one man and one woman. A man and woman who are married to each other. God forbids all sex outside of marriage, including adultery.*

Some women asked about sex toys—devices used to artificially enhance sexual pleasure. I don't know much about these, but I do know that using them can become addictive, can cause pain and injury, and can replace or ruin sexual intimacy with your spouse. Besides, the people who manufacture these items are very often involved in the world of prostitution, pornography, drugs, and even worse. My advice is to steer clear of these things.

Many women also expressed the opinion that pornography has no place in a marriage. "I think a lot of people bring it into their marriage," one woman said, "but I feel like that's the same as bringing other people into it." I agree wholeheartedly.

Many couples mistakenly believe that viewing porn together (magazines, videos, Internet) will turn them on and make sex more arousing and exciting. This may be true at first, but there's a catch. Porn is powerfully addictive and, over time, you'll get desensitized. It will take harder and harder porn to turn you on. And more likely than not, during sex, one or both of you will be fantasizing about someone other than your spouse.

Sex isn't just about creating the best possible physical sensation. It's about creating intimacy with the man you married. Porn pollutes holy, intimate, God-given sex by inviting Satan to the party.

Sex by Yourself

What about masturbation? This one's a bit of a split decision among Christians. Some say it's always wrong because it leaves your mate out of the equation. Others say it's okay at certain times with your mate's

---

* See 1 Corinthians 7:2; Matthew 5:32.

blessing. When your husband is out of town on business for two weeks, for example.

I'm not sure how I feel about it, to be honest. But one thing I do know is that if you're masturbating without your husband's blessing, I don't think it can bring anything but harm to your marriage.

Here's Trina's story:

"I started masturbating when my husband and I were engaged. I have never told a soul about this, so it is not easy. I would stimulate my nipples and rub up against a pillow I had placed between my legs. When I got married and started having sex, it didn't feel half as good as the orgasms I could have on my own. So I kept masturbating whenever my husband was away. I always felt so guilty afterward and would swear I'd never do it again. But I always did.

"When he wanted sex, I was never in the mood. I didn't even want him touching me. It got pretty bad, and our marriage suffered, but I was addicted to my habit and couldn't stop.

"My story has a happy ending. God showed me I was destroying my marriage with my selfishness. After a few months of intense prayer, and finding a godly (female) accountability partner, I finally conquered the beast. It took a while before sex felt good, but it does now. And my marriage is so much better.

"I would strongly urge young women to stay away from masturbating. It's just not worth it."

True Freedom

There is certainly great freedom in being sexually flexible and willing to experiment in new ways in the bedroom. It can take your entire relationship to a new level. The important thing is to communicate with each other and to practice unselfishness on a daily basis.

"You, my brothers, were called to be free," Paul writes in Galatians. "But do not use your freedom to indulge the sinful nature; rather, serve one another in love."

Freedom brings with it responsibility—for yourself and for others. Freedom doesn't mean doing whatever we want, whenever we want—though that's our typical view of the term. True freedom is never about ourselves in isolation. True freedom is viewed through the lens of consideration for others.

"Holy sex is about loving, not using," Dr. Gardner says, "and it is about unity much more than it is about fun." Don't try stuff just because you think the world is on to something that you're missing. Do things you honestly like—or that your husband likes—not things you feel you should like because "everybody else does it."

The decision to have oral sex and how frequently to do it is totally up to you as a couple. Does every guy like it? I can't answer that. To your average Joe, I would guess it feels incredibly good physically. But because guys love to watch their woman get pleasure, it probably doesn't give him the *emotional* delight that bringing her to orgasm during intercourse does.

If your hubby would love an occasional "treat," but you don't like oral sex, examine your motives. Ask yourself, "Why don't I like it?" Too much effort with too little return for *me*? If hubby genuinely loves it, would doing it occasionally as a willing gesture of loving service put me out too much?

Make the choice that's right for *your* marriage, whatever that choice may be.

Chapter 12

The Eyes of Men

Men are visual. We women know this. And it drives us nuts. On the one hand, it's kind of nice knowing we can turn our hubbies on by our appearance alone. On the other hand, so can any other woman who walks in front of him or across the television screen.

It's easy to get discouraged, frustrated, even furious at our husbands for their visual nature. It would be great if I was the most beautiful woman on earth and my husband had eyes only for me. But I'm not. And he doesn't.

So, what can we wives do to help guard our husbands' eyes from sexual temptation?

Do you want to hand this book to your man while I stomp up to my podium and yell at him to unglue his eyeballs from that cleavage-baring floozy at the football game, that hot young thing on his favorite TV show, or his best friend's gorgeous, curvy wife? Would you like me to give him a piece of my mind? Shall I threaten him within an inch of his life never to look at—or even think about—another woman again, save you, his lovely wife?

I'd better not. This book, after all, is for us women, not our husbands. And even if it weren't, that in-your-face approach would not go over so well. It would cause more problems than it would solve, more likely than not.

So again, what can we wives do?

I asked some of my close friends to share some suggestions for encouraging our husbands to stay pure. They had a lot of great input and helped me come up with four things we can do to proactively help our husbands in this area:

1. Pray—seek God first.
2. Monitor what you both watch.
3. Stay attractive—care about your appearance.
4. Satisfy him sexually (the "sex solution").

Seek God First

As cliché as it may sound, soaking the matter in a daily prayer bath is the first, and singly most important, thing. Each day ask God to keep your husband's eyes from wandering, to keep his thoughts pure, and to keep him attracted to *you*. Ask God to show you each day something you can do to lessen your husband's struggles in this area.

You don't have a lot of control over a husband who doesn't want to change, but *God* does. Faithfully take it to Him, and trust Him to answer your prayers in His perfect timing. Then patiently wait for Him.

"I am convicted to pray daily that God will guard my husband," my friend Jodie says. "We need to be willing to put on the full armor of God and battle the enemy over our husbands."

I'm so thankful that Gabe has never been one to gaze at other women or let his tongue hang out during racy commercials. He's never flirtatious with my friends and doesn't turn on the charm around the opposite sex. After talking honestly with a couple girlfriends whose husbands have battled addiction to pornography, I never realized how good I had it.

But I knew Gabe had to be attracted to other women to *some* degree. So last week I sat him down and asked him some tough questions.

In a nutshell, he said that of course he notices beautiful women, but he realizes he's been given an incredible gift in a wife who loves him, daughters who love him, and a relationship with the Lord. Why in the world would he throw away that gift?

Wow. Can you say "blessed"? If your husband does a good job of keeping his eyes only on you, he deserves all the love and affection you can possibly lavish on him. I need to remind myself of this fact on a daily basis.

I've come to the conclusion that those men who are more emotional and passionate about life and people (often those in ministry) are more likely to struggle with lust. Men who are quieter, more logical, less boisterous, less apt to hug people impulsively, are less likely to have trouble in this area. Of course, there are always exceptions.

So, if you've found yourself wishing your husband were more eloquent or passionate, be thankful for the trade-off. He very well may be more inclined to faithfulness—with his eyes and mind, and in real life too.

If your husband struggles with wandering eyes, pray that God will convict him to strive to make *you* his sole source of sexual stimulation. Then take it one step further. Ask your husband what *you* can do to make this a reality.

Each day, we wives should be thinking, *What can I do today to help build a protective fence around my precious marriage?*

Watch What You Watch

One step we can take is to monitor what we watch on television and in movies. It's hard for a man not to think sexual thoughts about other women if he's constantly taking in visual images of sexy female bodies.

Gabe and I have a rule: no R-rated movies. We do make exceptions—war/action movies rated R for violence are sometimes allowed to make our list. What we don't want to see is a movie rated R for sexual content.

One night last summer we broke our rule, and I've regretted it ever since. We had a babysitter for our girls, and I wanted to see a romantic comedy, go to dinner, and then come home and have sex. *Wedding Crashers* was the only film showing in that particular genre at the time.

It was rated R. It turned out that the R was for *raunchy*. Sex was the premise of the entire film.

One sequence involved a series of two-second clips of closeups on naked women's breasts—about ten or so different women falling back on a bed and squealing.

When Gabe lowered his eyes in embarrassment, I should have grabbed my popcorn and walked out the door. He even asked me if I wanted to leave. "No," I told him. "It's okay. Maybe that's the worst of it."

But it wasn't. As we left the movie and headed to the restaurant, I felt sick to my stomach. How was I going to have sex with all those images of busty women flashing through my head? And who knew what was going on in Gabe's mental images file?

We ended up having a great talk over burgers. We agreed that sex scenes in movies make lousy foreplay. And we remembered why we made our rule in the first place.

"Scantily clad women make me mad," my friend Daphne says candidly. To that I would add, "And bare-breasted women make me even madder."

"I hate how this world has polluted our minds," my friend Jodie says. "TV is trash. Computers are polluted with pornography. I think it is wise to make sure we avoid visual stimuli. I also think it is important to provide 'visual pleasure' for your husband by making an effort to look good and appealing to him occasionally."

Both Jodie and Daphne feel it is important to offer accountability and support to our husbands when it comes to what they're viewing on-screen, be it movies, TV, or the Internet.

"I periodically check up on my husband to make sure he's been pure with what he's been looking at on the Internet," Daphne notes. "He knows I'm doing it, and it keeps him accountable. It also eases my mind (he always tells the truth) so I don't worry about him or think he's hiding something."

I think this is good. Work out an agreement with your husband. It's not about "I don't trust you." It's about "I want to be your loving accountability partner."

Care About Your Appearance

I haven't always done the best job taking care of myself physically. And now that our last baby has been born and I'm 30 (30!), I'm feeling the need to start.

In her book *For Women Only,* Shaunti Feldhahn has a great chapter entitled, "The Truth About the Way You Look." She talks about how important a wife's appearance is to her husband. Many of them don't express their feelings, however, because they don't want to hurt their wives' feelings.

"Most of us can get paralyzed into inaction by the thought of having to look like the impossibly thin twenty-year-olds on TV," Shaunti says, but what men consistently told her was that "the effort to take care of herself for him" was what mattered most, not shrinking down to fit into that honeymoon bikini from yesteryear.

I actually do have a friend whose husband told her recently that if she still looked good in her honeymoon bikini when she turned 50, he would buy her any car she wanted. This couple hasn't yet started a family, but they insist they want five kids in five years. I wish her the best, but I truly hope her husband will show some grace and buy her that car anyway.

Shaunti reports one man's candid comment on women who pack on the pounds after the wedding. "Those women need to realize that their doubling in size is like a man going from being a corporate raider to a minimum-wage slacker—and assuming it has no effect on his spouse."

We women might argue there is a double standard when it comes to upkeep of physical appearance after tying the knot. I don't disagree. Many men gain lots of weight in the years following their wedding. And as a general rule, it *is* more socially acceptable for a man to be overweight than a woman.

Is this fair? No. But remember, we're not so much about what's *fair* in this book as what's *right.* More specifically, doing what's right ourselves and counting on *God* to work on our husbands.

And truthfully, while our man's appearance is important to us, there are probably many things higher on our list. Like providing for us financially. Giving us affection. Being romantic. Showing that he loves us. Spending time with us.

Because of a man's visual nature, your appearance ranks higher on *his* list than his appearance does on *yours.* The desire your husband has for you to look good is a legitimate desire.

In addition to a visual nature, men are born with an ingrained competitiveness. As barbaric as it may sound, there's an unspoken competition going on—who got himself a good-looking wife? Guys want to be proud of their wives. They want other men to slap them on the back and say, "Nice going, dude. Nice catch."

I asked a few of my friends what steps they've taken to look attractive for their husbands. "I color my hair, swim for exercise, control my eating (ouch!), and wear clothes he likes," Wendy said.

"I try to listen to him," Jodie told me. "I know he likes my hair long. He requests certain clothes. It is important to learn what your husband likes and try to please him. I love to surprise him with dim lights and get all dressed up in heels and a little dress or something nice. Women can get so lazy and fat. I think it is important to try to stay fit, healthy, and conscious of your appearance."

"In a way, this issue for men is like the romance issue for us," Shaunti Feldhahn says. "We love him regardless, but it doesn't salve the empty wistfulness we feel or the pain we may suffer wondering why on earth our man doesn't see that this is so important to us."

Wives may be muttering, "I shouldn't have to *do* all these things just to keep my husband loving me. He should love me unconditionally."

But at the same time, husbands are grumbling, "I shouldn't have to *do* things—show affection, listen to her drawn-out stories, quit passing gas—just to keep my wife loving me. She should love me unconditionally."

It works both ways, ladies. You chose to get married. You wanted a husband. Loving unconditionally and unselfishly means doing things that aren't always easy but will make your husband happy. And remember, most men just want to know you care enough about *them* to make an effort. Not perfection, just an *effort.*

Let your appearance make the statement, "I care enough about you to provide you with a wife who is pleasing to your eyes. I care enough about you to help you keep your eyes off other women and on me."

Now, if your husband is overly obsessed (in a negative way) with your body and your failure to meet his standards, pray. Do all you can (within reason) to be attractive for him—as long as your convictions aren't compromised. If he wants you to lose 30 pounds—and you agree that you really need to—try your best to do it. If his requests are selfish and unreasonable, you don't have to give in. Ask God to show your husband the error of his ways.

An Interview with Daphne

My friend Daphne is great for speaking candidly about issues that are near and dear to her heart, so I sat down with her and asked her some things about her appearance and how it relates to "The Eyes of Men."

What do you think is your responsibility, as a wife, to help your husband fight impure thoughts?

"I used to get mad at men who wanted their wives to be thinner, but I've kind of changed my thinking on the subject. We should love our husbands unconditionally, whether they meet our emotional and romantic needs or not. But it sure would be nice if they did, wouldn't it? Wouldn't it make you feel loved? So if men are visual and they want their wives to look good, isn't that something we as wives can do for our husbands? They shouldn't love us any less if we are overweight, but out of love for them and desire to make them happy, shouldn't we try?"

It's obvious that you put time and effort into your appearance. You look great! What are some practical steps you've taken to stay attractive?

"Thanks. I try to eat nutritious food and not too much junk. I exercise often (not every day) and work on problem areas (firming my rear end). When trying to decide what clothes to keep and which ones to get rid of, I ask my husband to pick out what he likes and doesn't like. He likes shirts with 'action in the collar,' so when shopping, I keep that in mind.

"Basically, we should want to look nice to show our husbands we love them. We will eventually get old and wrinkly, our breasts will sag, we will have extra skin on our tummies from bearing children, and our metabolism will shut down—things that should make us beautiful because of a life well-lived. We will never look like the airbrushed models on TV, but I think we should make an effort to look good with what we have."

Do you ever get frustrated when you don't measure up to those "airbrushed models"?

"I struggle with wanting to be perfectly beautiful for my husband, but there is no such thing. It's something I must constantly take before God—that I would realize my beauty is from within. I would rather be a loving and giving wife than be a terrible grouch who is thin and beautiful on the outside. But discipline is a spiritual quality—and one I really want to possess."

The Sex Solution

When I asked Gabe what I could do to keep him from sexual temptation outside of our marriage, he answered without hesitation, "Initiate sex more."

Seems that if a man is sexually satisfied at home, he won't be looking or longing for it elsewhere. Now that's a concept. It's not a fail-proof guarantee, but it has quite a high success rate.

"It is imperative that women seek to understand and guard their husbands' sexual purity," my friend Jodie says with conviction. "I'm sick of women being selfish and sweeping their husbands' needs under the rug. Sure, we women are busy. Sure, our husbands don't always help or sympathize with us. But why are we so oblivious to their needs? We need to provide them with sexual fulfillment and pleasure."

Preach it, sister!

"I try really hard to keep my body desirable for my husband and only him," my friend Holly says. "I try to keep him sexually satisfied so he isn't tempted. Every three days is a good gauge for when a man *needs* sex."

What a privilege we have to help relieve sexual temptation for our husbands. It shouldn't be something we do just to keep our husband from pouting. By happily making love, we can help our husbands stay holy. That's a cool thought.

One final note of importance: No one likes a jealous wife—the clingy, whiny, threatening sort of gal who keeps her husband on a leash and whips him if he gets out of line.

But there *is* a *good* kind of jealousy. The Bible tells us that God is a jealous God—jealousy being defined as wanting for yourself what is *rightfully yours alone.* We belong to God, not Satan, and God will jealously fight the adversary for our souls.

It's okay to be possessive of your husband—provided you go about it the right way. Marriage was designed for the two of you alone. Your husband rightfully belongs to you.

"Godly jealousy means that you do your utmost to keep your spouse's attention focused on you. In as many ways as possible, you protect your spouse from any temptation to be unfaithful," says Tommy Nelson.

Let's purpose in our hearts to do whatever we can to protect our husbands and our marriages.

ADDING LITTLE ONES TO THE MIX

Chapter 13

Trying to Conceive

We're not pregnant yet, but we're sure having fun trying!"

A woman once shared those words with me, and I assume they were heartfelt. But I couldn't relate. For me, trying to make a baby took all the fun out of making love.

We had been married a little less than two years when we decided to put away the birth control and start a family. I can still feel the butterflies that fluttered in my stomach when I tossed the remainder of my pill pack in the trash can. I was ready to make unprotected love!

What would it be like having sex and conceiving a child? Pure, unadulterated joy, I thought. We would come together in a moment of exultant passion, Gabe's sperm would determinedly swim to my egg, and voilà! I'd be pregnant! I'd lie back and bask in the glow of my first few minutes of motherhood.

Yeah, right. We started trying in August. No baby. Just a period. Tried again in September. Period. October. Period. November, December, January. February. Lots of tears. Lots of frustration. But still no baby.

After the first couple months of negative pregnancy tests, a disturbing pattern developed. We'd have sex three or four days in a row during the time I thought I was most fertile, and then I couldn't have cared less if we made love the rest of the month.

Gabe began to feel gypped—like I was just using him to get a baby. Imagine that.

I was stressed. He was stressed. Our marriage was stressed. Time and time again—silently, out loud, and in my journal—I poured out my heart to God.

A Cry to God

"Lord, I've become way too familiar with terms like cervical mucus and basal body temperature. It all sounds so cold and technical, but what I'm feeling is so deep and emotional. Why can't this be easier for me? Why do I have to spend so much time and effort calculating this and that? And when it's all said and done, I'm still not pregnant!

"I'm tired of forcing lovemaking into a strict and impersonal box. I feel like my love life is on the clock—and the clock is ticking faster and faster.

"I just don't get it. Lord, I thought making a baby would be such a beautiful experience. The first month we tried was perfect. We made love four times in one week, and it was so special. I just knew we had conceived a baby out of our sensuous passion.

"Now, months later, the passion is long gone. It's more like a factory, an assembly line. Do this. Check that. Chart this. Take that. Make love. Then again.

"Lord, is it too much to ask to restore the beauty and passion to this baby-making process? Is there any way you could help me just to relax? Should I put away the ovulation predictor sticks and just trust You?

"And I'm worried about Gabe, Lord. This is hard on him, too, though for a different reason than it is for me. I'm upset because I want a baby so badly. I think he's really struggling with the stress this is putting on our sex life. And our marriage in general.

"I know I'm being a crappy wife. Please help me, God!"

A Delight Becomes a Chore

Carrie can feel my pain. She and her husband John have been trying for most of their marriage (over five years) to have a baby. She explains how trying to conceive has put a damper on their once-exciting sex life.

"When we were first married, it was any time of the day or night and *very* often," she recalls. "We'd even come home from work for lunch and have sex then. We have now been trying to conceive for five years, and we pretty much have sex around the time I'm ovulating and not much more. It's become more of a chore at times. And, now it's only ever at night right before bed. Never morning or afternoon sex—or middle-of-the-night sex. We used to do that, too."

Carrie went on to tell me that having to have sex at certain times "even if we are tired or sick or just don't feel like it" makes sex so much less enjoyable.

John used to initiate sex all the time. His sexual appetite was far more voracious than Carrie's. Now Carrie can't remember the last time John asked her to make love. She's the one who suggests it 100 percent of the time, and it's really frustrating for her when John doesn't make an effort to be an active participant in their lovemaking.

I am not a guy, so I can't pretend to know exactly what John is feeling. Perhaps he feels less of a man, knowing that, these days, Carrie is only interested in sex when there's a chance of making a baby. Maybe he longs for those days when he felt Carrie's desire for him and knew she wasn't "using" him to get pregnant.

Perhaps this whole infertility thing has made him question his masculinity. *Why can't I get my wife pregnant? What's wrong with me?*

Helping Your Husband

When you're having difficulty conceiving a child, you have two huge problems swirling around in your life: 1) You desperately want a baby and don't have one. And 2) Your husband is feeling neglected (and rightfully so).

What are you going to do? Well, to be honest, there is very little you can do about the baby part. Only God can create life, and He will do it in His perfect timing. In the words of Psalm 37, "Be still before the Lord and wait patiently for him."

Look for verses that speak of God's comfort and—as tough as it may be—try to take them to heart. Here's one to get you started:

> Don't fret or worry. Instead of worrying, pray. Let petitions and praises shape your worries into prayers, letting God know your concerns. Before you know it, a sense of God's wholeness, everything coming together for good, will come and settle you down. It's wonderful what happens when Christ displaces worry at the center of your life.*

So do your best to put your baby-to-be in God's hands, and focus on something you *can* do—please your husband. If you neglect your husband's needs during this time, he is less apt to be emotionally supportive of you when you need him most.

Even if your husband wants a baby himself, it might be hard for him to understand just how *badly* you want one. God has infused us women with an innate desire to become a mother to a child. The parenting instinct just isn't as strong for most men—at least at this point.

Your husband is not being selfish or insensitive. He just doesn't understand. Be patient with him. And like I said—meet his needs, and he'll be more willing to sympathize with yours.

Your man might also have a real, and common, fear—that a child will take his place in your heart and life. If he feels that this child has already displaced him, and it hasn't even been conceived yet, it could be very depressing for him. Even if he feels secure in your love, he might not feel secure in the fact that you'll still be devoted to meeting his sexual needs once a baby comes into the picture.

The realization that he alone cannot make you happy—that you need someone else to complete and fulfill you—can be a tough pill for your husband to swallow.

If you haven't read Hannah's story in 1 Samuel 1, here's a brief excerpt. (I urge you to read the whole thing.) We find Hannah weeping over her inability to have a child, and her husband Elkanah says to her, "Hannah,

---

* Philippians 4:6-7 MSG.

why are you weeping? Why don't you eat? Why are you downhearted? Don't I mean more to you than ten sons?"

We don't get to hear Hannah's response, but we know she had a choice to make. She could continue to weep and wallow in her misery and lash out at her husband for his ignorance and insensitivity. Or she could assure him of her love for him. Some good sex (while she's not ovulating) would probably do the trick.

You will need extra strength during this time to willingly and excitedly make love to your husband—yes, even when you're not midway through your cycle—but God will willingly and excitedly give it to you if you ask.

It is vitally important to the health and future of your marriage that you not neglect your husband during this challenging season of your life.

The Rest of My Story

We tried for eight months before I got pregnant with our first child. (A mere blip on the radar screen of life for some couples like John and Carrie, who have been trying for years.) And wouldn't you know it—our baby was conceived during one of the few times we made love without "trying."

Our second baby took all of ten minutes to conceive, so that was a nice break.

Our third took ten months, then we had a miscarriage just a week after we found out I was expecting. Six weeks later, we got pregnant again with a healthy baby. That little one is occupying my womb as I type.

I vividly remember one night sometime during the year we were trying to make baby number three. I approached Gabe and asked him if he wanted to make love.

"You're ovulating again *already?*" he asked, surprised.

"No, I'm not ovulating."

"You're *not* ovulating?"

"Nope."

"Did you just get *done* ovulating? Are you *about* to ovulate?"

"Nope and nope."

"Is there any chance you could get pregnant tonight?"

"Maybe one in a million."

"Then why do you want to have sex?"

My heart sank. It had immediately become obvious I had been neglecting his needs.

"Uh, just to have sex?"

When he realized I was serious, his face relaxed into an impish little grin.

"Well, I'll be! Let's go!"

It wasn't that hard to go the extra mile to meet his needs. And once Gabe saw I was willing to do that, he developed a much more positive attitude toward me and the baby we would someday conceive.

We've decided this baby is our last, and while I feel a twinge of sadness knowing we'll never create another baby together again, the sense of relief I feel is even stronger. No more months of trying to conceive. No more sex just when I'm ovulating. From now on, sex is just about us—not any other human being.

I love getting pregnant, being pregnant, and having babies. But I'm ready to move on—and so is my husband.

When You're Finally Pregnant

Once you get pregnant, especially if it took you a long time, the temptation to abstain from sex for the next nine months is very real.

"Why would I have sex now?" you ask. "There's no need. Besides, I worked so hard to get pregnant. I deserve a break!"

A couple weeks ago, I was in a room of mixed company when someone brought up my latest book, which happened to be this one.

Gabe explained it was for women only and it was about sex. For some reason, he loves telling people about this particular project of mine. It's like he's adopted it as his own.

I cautiously shared that my hope for the book was to help women realize how important sex is to a happy, healthy marriage.

Our friend Rick's eyes lit up. "Sherri needs to read your book," he said, with a pointed look at his very pregnant wife.

"Hey, I'm pregnant, aren't I?" she retorted. "So, you must be getting some!"

Ouch. I knew where this was heading.

"Yeah, I got some seven months ago," he replied, "and none since."

As much as I love to be in the middle of a couple's public argument about their lack of sex (ha!), I abruptly changed the subject.

But I really felt for Rick. I knew Sherri had waited a long time to be a mommy, and she was going to be a wonderful one, but I was afraid that she had finally gotten what she really wanted, and Rick's needs and desires were being put on the back burner…or shoved off the stove altogether.

I once heard a woman say, "Give him sex so he'll give you kids. That's all we women really want anyway."

Girls, don't ever, ever listen to this kind of advice. It's selfish—and unbiblical. Adopting an attitude like that will only make your marriage suffer. And ironically, your children will suffer as well—those same children you've deliberately placed above your husband on the family totem pole.

Your Baby Will Thank You

If you've read the previous 12 chapters in this book, then I don't need to tell you again how important it is to meet your husband's sexual needs. Even while you're pregnant.

Now, having been pretty nauseated during my first trimester with all of my pregnancies, I know how tough it can be to stomach the thought of having sex during that time. But if at all possible, do it whenever you can. Or at least find a time of day when you feel well enough to give hubby a good hand job.

And once your morning sickness (or all-day sickness, if we're being realistic) has passed, and as long as you're not a high-risk pregnancy with a doctor's orders to abstain from sex, there's no reason why you can't resume your previous lovemaking schedule.

Now, I know there are exceptions. My dear friend Missy spent two entire pregnancies vomiting constantly. During her second nine-month round, she was hooked up to an IV for 20 hours a day. If you can relate to her prenatal experience, consider yourself exempt from this section of the chapter.

Now, back to the rest of us. Pregnant women (myself included) tend to believe that the world revolves around them. We think about ourselves and our babies constantly. In our minds, our husbands cease to have their own needs and exist solely to meet ours. We need a milkshake, a

In Sickness and in Health

Unfortunately, illness isn't confined to pregnancy. Many a marriage has endured a brief—or extended—period where either the husband or wife is unable to make love due to sickness or injury.

We often take our good health for granted, until it's gone. And it's hard to be adequately prepared for the strain a prolonged illness can put on your marriage.

One couple I know went through a particularly tough year while the wife battled mononucleosis. She barely had enough energy to even function, let alone have sex. Her husband loved her deeply but became increasingly frustrated, even hurt and angry at times.

"Looking back," he says, "I still feel sorrowful when I think of that 'lost year' in our relationship." But their marriage survived and is now thriving, and he adds, "Because of what we went through, we're able to be more patient, supportive, and understanding with each other now when we have to face physical challenges."

Illness and injuries are thieves that can quickly steal the joy out of our marriages—if we let them. I'm in no position to offer advice for a situation I've not (yet) experienced, but I am convinced that God knows your pain. He loves you deeply and wants you to lean on Him during difficult times like these, whether it's you that is sick or your spouse.

Pour out your heart to Him in prayer, spend time reading your Bible, and—especially important—look for counsel and encouragement from someone with experience and godly advice.

Life can be tough, and the answers aren't always easy to come by, but thankfully, we don't have to go through life's trials on our own.

foot rub, some pickles at three in the morning, a back scratch, a glass of water, a neck rub...

We want to perpetually prattle about our pregnancy and baby. And we want our husbands to listen. And nod. And offer words of affection and encouragement. How can they think about sex at a time like this? Everything else in the world should pale in comparison to the baby we are carrying in utero.

Girls, let me tell you something. If you want your husband to be a good father, you need to be a good wife. A man who is well taken care of by his wife (in bed and out) will naturally be a more loving father than a man whose wife neglects his needs.

Think of how you would feel if he were the one who was pregnant and getting all the attention. I'd probably be more than a little resentful.

By all means, enjoy this beautiful, miraculous, and fleeting stage of your life. And include your hubby in as many aspects of it as you can. But remember, while he's meeting your emotional needs, meet his sexual ones.

Someday (in about 20 or 30 years), your baby will thank you. And keep in mind that once that baby enters the world, it becomes ten times tougher to make sex a priority than when you were pregnant. You might not believe me now, but trust me. Every other mother on the planet will back me up on this one.

Fringe Benefits

In case no one has ever told you, pregnant sex can be some of the most erotic and exciting sex you'll ever have—in your second trimester, anyway.

For one thing, your body fills up with tons more blood than you usually have, and all your sexual organs become engorged—like they do when you're aroused. If you're anything like me, orgasms come quicker and more powerfully than they do at any other time. When I'm pregnant, I even have vivid dreams about sex sometimes and wake up wanting my hubby.

And if you weren't blessed with a billowing bust, your new pregnant boobs can enhance your sex life like you wouldn't believe—after they get over their initial soreness. When I forget about my largeness everywhere else and just focus on my new voluptuous breasts, I feel extremely feminine and sexy. And we all know that when a woman *feels* sexy, she *is* sexy.

Yes, comfortably positioning your bodies can be challenging as your middle grows larger by the minute (try sitting on your husband's lap facing away from him), but it's a challenge well worth taking on.

Believe you me, you don't want to miss out on some of the best months of loving you and your hubby might ever know!

On Second Thought...

In my quest to be candid, I feel the need to share a postscript to the above paragraphs I wrote before I hit the eight-month mark in my pregnancy. Gabe and I are this close to swearing off intercourse completely until my six-week postpartum checkup.

Why? Well, to be frank, our last five or six lovemaking experiences have ended in disaster.

Ever been seconds away from orgasm when suddenly your clitoris decided it was overstimulated and became excruciatingly painful to the touch?

Ever been seconds away from orgasm and get a cramp on your right side that rivaled intense labor pains without medication?

Ever finished making love and been unable to walk for 24 hours afterward because your crotch was throbbing like a period gone terribly wrong?

We'll keep trying, but there's no guarantee we'll be successful. At the very least, I'll buck up, reread "Oral Delights" from Dr. Leman's book, and put some of those great ideas to good use. There's nothing like practicing what I preach!

Chapter 14

Baby Makes Three

Many a married couple goes through their first pregnancy totally oblivious to the fact that the birth of their child is going to completely rock their world—their marriage in particular. Oh, plenty of people have tried to warn them, but they naively believed that they'd be different, the exception to the rule.

I can hear them now…"Parenthood will be perfectly blissful. With the love we'll feel for our new shared creation, how could our marriage do anything but blossom and grow?"

Blossom, schlossom.

You'll have to excuse me for sounding so cynical. Believe me, it's all in fun. With a touch of seriousness. I have yet to meet a husband and wife who were truly prepared for the impact that parenthood would have on their relationship.

I'm not suggesting you should adopt a doomsday attitude. No need.

And I'm not saying that entering the world of parenting with your husband by your side is not a fabulous phenomenon wrought with possibility. It is.

I am merely pointing out that parenthood is a huge adjustment. It will require much work, sacrifice, and unselfishness to keep your marriage running smoothly once you add the "Mommy" hat to your growing collection. And you reserve the right not to believe me until it actually happens to you.

No two women are alike when it comes to making the transition from wife to mommy/wife. How you handle things will depend on a myriad of factors—your personality, your husband's temperament, the state of your marriage, how long you've been married, your experience with children, the ease/difficulty of your pregnancy and childbirth, your child, and so on. But, no matter how different we are, we can all learn helpful tips from each other.

As long as we're careful to offer advice from experience, not idealism.

Case in point: A few weeks ago, my friend Kellyn, fresh from the birthing trenches for the third time, was visiting with a married-without-children friend. Kellyn was sharing how hard it was to give her husband much time and affection with two toddlers and a newborn demanding her attention.

"You know, Kellyn," this "friend" admonished, "Your marriage needs to come first. And then you can tend to your children."

Um, okay. Bad move, sister. Nothing gets my goat like "helpful" advice from people who have never walked a step in my shoes. Her advice is right on the mark—don't get me wrong. Your marriage *should* come first. But she would do well to zip her lips until she has earned the right to preach on certain topics.

I put off writing this chapter until a time when I could write with true empathy. My third child was born a whopping 13 days ago. If that doesn't qualify me to wax eloquent on the topic, I don't know what would.

Since sex and marriage are the focus of this book, I won't be divulging helpful tips for changing diapers or curing colic. This chapter will hone in on ways to meet your baby's needs without neglecting your hubby.

Yes, there will be times when your husband will have to live with less sex—the nauseating first trimester of pregnancy, the six weeks you're recovering from childbirth, the days when you've nursed your newborn until your nipples nearly fell off. But we can't use these seasons as an excuse to ignore our husbands' sexual needs. No matter how crazy hectic life seems to be.

Let's look at some of the main problems we'll face as the lover and new mom in us collide:

- I'm sooo tired.
- I have no desire.
- I'm fat.
- I'm depressed.
- He doesn't understand.
- I'm trying to be Superwoman.

Now we'll tackle them one at a time.

I'm Sooo Tired!

"There are days when I'm so tired I don't have enough energy for sex," Lindsey says.

"We hardly ever have sex because I am too tired from being up with the baby," echoes Jamie.

"Babies change everything," says Liz. "They demand so much time and energy. I feel so incredibly tired, disorganized, and frustrated at times."

Did you know that during your child's first year of life, you will lose between 400 and 750 hours of sleep? (Lorilee Craker reports this disheartening fact.) That is a stinkin' lot of sleep!

Unless you share baby duty equally, you, the mom, are probably the one losing the most shuteye. This lack of snooze-time can be seriously detrimental to your love life.

"You're not going to drive off the side of the road and hit a phone pole if you haven't had enough sex," Lorilee jokes in *We Should Do This More Often*, "but you just might if you don't sleep enough."

Suggestions for getting sleep *and* making love all in one week? Get some help if you can—someone who can love on your baby for awhile so you can take a two-hour afternoon nap.

Let some of your household chores go. We often seem to make time for dishes and laundry but not for sex. Ask your husband which would mean more to him—20 minutes of sex or an empty sink?

Ask God for strength. The Creator and Sustainer of the universe has proven He is more than capable of making something out of nothing. "I am the Lord, the God of all mankind," He tells us in the book of Jeremiah. "Is anything too hard for me?"

Just the other night, Gabe was craving some intercourse-alternative intimacy, and I was desperately craving nothing more than a couple hours of precious sleep.

If it weren't for the convicting power of writing a book about sex, I probably would have stared him down and started spouting off—"Dream on, mister! Do you have *any* idea how exhausted I am? Why don't *you* get up six times every night and nurse and change a crying newborn? *Then* tell me how much sex you want!"

In an attempt to avoid hypocrisy, I practiced what I've been preaching. With as cheerful an attitude as I could muster, keeping the nasty words to myself. And when it was all said and done, I was no worse for wear. And my hubby was deeply grateful. It was well worth the effort.

"I went through a very tough time of feeling selfish and frustrated after our baby was born," my friend Liz says. "I was tired, but didn't want to enlist the help of my husband or anyone to manage my baby. I didn't communicate how I was feeling and didn't care how he felt. My time with God was at a minimum...basically I just complained to God every night at two o'clock about how lazy my husband was. The Lord has been changing me and my heart. Selfishness hurts everyone...including yourself!"

Many women, sadly, welcome the relief that babies bring. "Ahhh... finally. Now I have a valid excuse to say no to sex." Bad attitude, girl.

We'll have sex more often when the kids get older and easier to take care of, I've found myself thinking. No, we won't. If we don't make love when my girls are 0, 3, and 4, we won't make love when they're 10, 13, and 14.

It *does* keep getting easier, as long as you start *right now,* when it's hard. You can't put it off for weeks or months and expect to get right back in the groove. Ask God for the strength to start *now.*

"He gives strength to the weary and increases the power of the weak…those who hope in the LORD will renew their strength," we read in Isaiah.

God will help you find energy where none should logically exist.

I Have No Desire!

Many women are surprised to find that tiredness aside, as new moms, they just don't have any physical desire to have sex.

I read something recently that I never knew. This explains a large part of the problem. Lorilee Craker explains it:

> Postpartum women are estrogen deprived because the placenta is no longer there. During pregnancy your placenta instead of your ovaries produces estrogen. And no estrogen equals not much desire.

When a woman breastfeeds, she usually doesn't ovulate for six months to a year after giving birth. Until those ovaries kick back into gear, estrogen and hence your sexual desire will be quite low.

Breastfeeding women also produce *prolactin*—a hormone that dries up natural lubricants and stops libido in its tracks. Plus, breastfeeding is so physically stimulating that it's often all the touching we need in any given day. And then some.

Breastfeeding is obviously a wonderful choice for your baby, but it can become an easy cop-out for neglecting our husbands, if we're not careful. Ask God to help you make wonderful choices for your husband as well—including when to give him back exclusive rights to your boobies.

Sometimes the only way to increase your desire is simply to have sex more often.

I'm Fat!

Some women shed pregnancy pounds in less than half the time it took them to pack them on. I know one woman who had her baby at the end of April, and by the first of June was back in her size-two pants and looking good.

Other women not only hang on to their "baby weight" but keep adding to it as the months go by. It isn't long before they weigh much more than they did right before they delivered.

"I feel unattractive physically because pregnancy has taken a toll," Erin says. "Any feelings of self-consciousness have doubled since pregnancy."

"After two children, I no longer have the body I did a few years ago," Dana says. "It is very distressing. I have never been this heavy before. I would rather have them in my life than not, but I can't stand the way I look after carrying them."

I was fortunate to lose all my pregnancy weight with my first two babies. Of course, you moms know that's only half the battle. What to do with the small, saggy breasts and the folds of skin around your middle that no longer have a home?

I'm not so naïve that I assume that I'll lose the weight that easily the third time around. I was much older this pregnancy and gained weight at a remarkably steady clip. I ate around the clock and stopped exercising around the five-month mark because I couldn't breathe. These last ten pounds don't seem to want to budge.

Fight the urge to compare yourself to women around you whose bodies don't seem phased even after multiple pregnancies. God never promises that all—or any—of life is fair.

It *is* important to get back in shape. Extra weight and lack of muscle tone only contribute to your fatigue. Yes, exercise takes energy, and you don't have a lot to spare. Just get started, and go easy at first. You'll find that exercise ultimately gives you *more* energy. Further, as Sheila Wray Gregoire explains,

> Energy has another important side effect: it increases our sex drives and makes it easier for us to experience sexual pleasure. Building muscle tone and endurance helps us "keep up" with sex, but cardio workouts also increase blood flow everywhere, making it easier to become, and stay, aroused.

Try to eat right whenever you can. Exhausted mommas often crave comfort food, but junk food will just make you sleepier. Eating healthy and exercising after baby are never easy, but you'll ultimately feel better about yourself, and your efforts will speak volumes to your husband.

The good news is that you are probably much more turned off by your postbaby body than your spouse is. Most hubbies delight in their wives' bodies no matter what.

I'm Depressed!

Nearly everyone experiences the baby blues to some degree after giving birth. No, it's not all in your head. And no, it doesn't mean you're a bad mom.

God gave us great bodies that recognize what's going on inside themselves and adjust accordingly. But when you've had a living, growing child dwelling and developing inside of you for nine months, and suddenly it's gone, your body and hormones can freak out.

Your body has to switch gears instantly, and that's not always easy. At least when you first got pregnant, it had time to adjust to the new life inside. The baby started out microscopic and slowly grew over a period of nine months. When you deliver—pow!—huge baby, 40 weeks in the works, poof! Just like that!

So your hormones are going to go a little wacky. Plus, you're tired, overwhelmed, confused, scared. There's a lot of new responsibility riding on your shoulders. And your life has been drastically disrupted.

If you were one of the haughty ones who insisted pre-baby that your life would stay the same once you had a child, you're eating your words right about now.

If your blues get so bad that you feel like life is too much for you, if you feel so depressed you could die, I gently yet strongly encourage you to get some help. It could be as simple as asking an older, godly woman to sit down and talk with you and pray with you. Maybe you could find a group of other new moms to spend time with.

If you need something more, like professional counseling or medication, don't hesitate to seek that out. You're not a wimp. You're doing what's best for you and your family. Remember—postpartum depression is *real*. And it can affect any one of us.

Pray to God for wisdom and make full use of whatever resources He sends your way.

He Doesn't Understand!

"You just don't understand!" you yell at your husband for the fourth time in one day. "You have no idea what I'm going through! What could *you* possibly know about being pregnant and giving birth and trying to nurse a colicky baby?"

Let's go easy on 'em, girls. Yes, we'd all love for our husbands to be understanding. Better yet, it'd be great if they could truly empathize with what we're going through, but they can't. And we shouldn't expect them to.

Liz and her husband worked through a difficult time after their baby was born. "I seemed distant at times," Liz says, "not because I was angry at him, but simply because I was exhausted. But he interpreted that to mean I wasn't interested in him. It was difficult for him. He wanted to be sensitive to me and my needs, yet longed to be sexually intimate to meet his needs."

There's a better option than deriding our husbands for their lack of understanding toward our plight. We can *pray* that God will give them some insight into and empathy for our situation.

When you yell at your husband for not understanding, it's not going to make him all the more determined to get it right next time. No, it will have the opposite effect. He'll just throw up his hands and quit trying all together. It's not worth the risk of failure in his estimation. When it comes to you, his odds of success probably seem rather slim.

Sending him on a guilt trip isn't fair. He's not a woman—and that's not his fault. He wasn't designed to experience the things you've experienced—or even to tackle many of the things you're tackling.

The phrase "*we're* pregnant" may be PC and all, but our hubbies really don't know what all this motherhood stuff is like. Don't be a whiner. Don't play the martyr. Humble yourself before God and ask Him for help.

If you've put your career on hold to stay at home with your little one, you may be feeling resentment toward your spouse, who still gets to interact with the real world.

Try not to blame your husband for your identity crisis. Tell yourself that your job as a mommy is easily the most important and valuable one you'll ever have. It's true. Don't underestimate the worth of what you're doing, just because you don't get a paycheck.

And remind yourself that these New Mommy Days are fleeting—no matter how endless the days and nights may seem right now.

I'm Trying to be Superwoman!

Sometimes—okay, always—we women want to do and have it all. We want healthy marriages, well-rounded and happy kids, a successful career, an effective ministry, fulfilling hobbies, and a well-kept home.

We *can* have it all, but more often than not, we can't have it all at once. We risk spreading ourselves too thin. Take it from someone who spends way too much time between the toast and the butter knife.

When you've got more than two handfuls of things and people you're trying to juggle, something is going to get dropped. And it will probably break. More than likely, your relationship (sexual or otherwise) with your husband will be the first to suffer.

We overextend ourselves and then society berates men for not picking up the slack at home. There's no rule that says your husband can't help out around the house and with the kids, but a home functions best when the heart of the home (you) isn't delegating all the responsibility of making the house homelike.

Your best bet is to put one or two (or more) things down on purpose so your juggling act will be easier, less stressful, less risky.

How do you know what to put down? You'll need to streamline. To simplify. To evaluate which things are most important. Which things you can't risk damaging or losing.

You may have to disappoint some people when they find out you can't (or aren't willing to) do it all. But your relationship with God, your husband, and your children—in that order—need to be put first. Then you can start adding other relationships and responsibilities one by one in order of their priority. Just make sure you stop before your life gets uncomfortably full.

If you're not sure what your limit is, ask your husband for his input and God for His divine wisdom, as the apostle James urges us.

It's tough being a great mom and a great anything-else at the same time. Don't try to do too much on top of your mothering. You'll wear yourself down quickly. Like I've already said, your baby's growing-up years will fly by, believe it or not, and there will be plenty of time later to fulfill other dreams and goals you might have.

This hits home for me as I struggle to get this book manuscript finished and sent off to the publisher. Look at me! I can write books and be a great mom all at once! Or not. The other day I was very frustrated

Balance, Not Breakdown

My friend Jodie is an accomplished marathon runner. Before Jodie had her first baby, she was able to successfully juggle her relationship with God and her husband, her nursing career, various ministries at church, and her marathon training.

Since baby Joanna was born nearly a year ago, Jodie has had to make some important decisions. "Balancing work, baby, hubby, church, and everything has been draining at times," she admits.

What balls should she put down before one or more of them gets dropped?

She cut her work week down to just two days, and her marathon training and races have taken a backseat. "I'm still running for exercise," Jodie says, "but I really miss the intense training. I feel like at least for now that I have to save up my energy for my husband and baby and God."

Sacrificing is never easy, but as Jodie realizes, she can always resume her career and marathon training full-time when her children are a little older. But if she were to try it all now, she'd probably either have a nervous breakdown or her marriage and children would suffer from damaging neglect. She's still able to be a nurse and a runner, just in smaller amounts of time.

that the baby was taking up every second of my day. "I'm not getting anything done!" I wailed.

"I'm probably going to make you mad by saying this," Gabe forewarned me, "but what do you really have to get done *right now*? Nina needs you. The other stuff can wait."

I was only mad for a second because he was right.

I'd imagine you're getting tired of hearing me say, "Pray about it," but I honestly feel like it's the first and best solution for every trouble. If you try your darnedest to be superwoman, you'll eventually fall flat on your face. Been there, done that. But when I admit my failures and ask God for strength, He supplies it every time.

The closer I am to God, the smaller everything else becomes. The converse is also true—the farther I roam from Him, the bigger my troubles seem.

When life is overwhelming me, it's because I'm not communing with God like I should. When I'm having an identity crisis, it's because I'm focusing on myself, not the Lord and my family.

Sex? Get Real!

"We have an infant, and lately, sex has been nearly impossible," Tammy says. "It never fails that as we get to the high point of the moment—or even get in the moment—the baby cries and romance flies out the door. It is hard to be in the mood when the background music is a screaming, teething baby."

Tammy isn't the only one whose sex life has taken a hit after the birth of a baby. The women I interviewed had plenty to say about the toll baby's first year took on their marriage.

So, we've established the fact that sex with Baby on Board is a daunting proposition. Now, what are we going to do to make sex a reality sometime before baby gets to high school?

The first thing that comes to mind is to get a babysitter. Now I realize that leaving your child with a babysitter for the first time can feel like your heart is being ripped out of your body. I spent half of our first date away from our firstborn sniffling away tears. I'm not suggesting that you do it immediately. There's no set age when you should leave your child for the first time. When your husband is ready is a good indicator. It's important for the health of your marriage that you spend some time away from your child on a regular basis. And it does get easier.

"Moms want to do their very best," says Lorilee Craker, "which, in a popular yet flawed line of thinking, means never leaving their babies for an instant, not even to spend time with the old sperm donor (er, father). Experts say that many of us overfeed the children and starve the marriage."

"I've learned to lean on the help of my precious mom," my friend Jodie told me. "Mom watches my baby at least one day a week. Even if I'm working it is a break, and I feel more rested for some reason."

What if a babysitter isn't an option for you at the moment? Elise has an idea for finding time for sex. "We just get started a little later, or leave her in the crib a while longer! I do find myself with less energy and that affects what kind of sex we have (quickie vs. foreplay)."

"I made a point to put our daughter in her crib at six weeks of age," Jodie says. "I try to be sure to keep our bedroom and bed reserved for *us*. I've learned to put Joanna to bed and turn my attention to my husband and to the Lord. I've learned to rest in the Lord and place my worries on His shoulders. This is a lesson that I need to learn over and over again."

I'm comforted by a verse in one of my all-time favorite Bible chapters, Isaiah 40. "He tends his flock like a shepherd: He gathers the lambs in his arms and carries them close to his heart; he gently leads those that have young."

God has a special place in His heart for moms of little ones. He knows the struggles we face, and he gently carries us through them. Praise Him!

It Can Be Done!

This is not a parenting book, and even if it were, there is much room for different parenting styles and philosophies within a biblical framework. When we start judging others for doing things differently than we do, we're not honoring God.

All I know is this: When you entered into a marriage covenant with your husband, you promised to love him with a Christ-like love through any circumstance, for as long as you both shall live. There is no "escape clause" for when a baby joins your family. As your husband's wife, you are still obligated, in God's eyes, to love and honor the man you married.

When you partner with God to fulfill that commitment, your relationship with the father of your child will deepen in ways you could never have imagined. It's not an easy balancing act, but it will be well worth it in the long run.

Yes, there will be times during baby's first year when your husband will have to go without sex. But do your best to make those stretches sweetly short. Ask God's help in putting your husband first. It won't be easy, but the rewards will be immeasurable.

Take it from someone who's been there three times.

When our third baby turned one month old, I felt ready to resume our sex life. No, I wasn't craving sex, but I had healed so nicely, and Gabe was being so wonderful that I knew it was time. We scheduled a time to make love, and I prayed all day beforehand. Then we prayed together in bed that God would bless our time together—and that the baby would stay asleep!

Yes, I was tired. But I was determined to 1) show Gabe how much I appreciated all his help and encouragement after Nina's birth and 2) be the lover he deserved, not just the mother of his daughters.

God answered my prayers. The night was a success (as were the second and third attempt). The fourth not so much. Crying baby, leaking breasts, ruined mood. Fifth time better than all the rest. And so on and so forth.

Making time for sex is admittedly difficult, but this young mom is determined to make it a priority. And just think—if I can make time for love (and actually enjoy it!) during this crazy season of my life, it can only keep getting better and better. Don't you think this can apply to just about everybody?

Chapter 15

Sex After Kids

I once had a woman turn her nose up at me for choosing to sit at home during a church roller-skating party.

Call me crazy for thinking it sounded like Chinese water torture to drag my two-year-old and six-month-old to a skating rink. They obviously couldn't skate, and I certainly couldn't *hold* either one of them while skating. I would have sat on a hard bench for three hours trying to entertain an infant and a toddler while keeping their tiny fingers out from under everybody's wheels.

Where again was the *fun* in all this?

"When *I* have kids," she informed me with disdain, "I'm not going to let them run my life!"

I offered no witty comeback. Not that I didn't have five or six really good ones burning a hole in the tip of my tongue, but none of them befit a professing Christian, so I kept my lips in lock mode. Besides, she was four months from her due date. Her first. If I could find a way to just bide my time, she'd be eating her words soon enough.

Twisting a biblical phrase just a bit, I have found it to be true that she who is without kids usually throws the first stone. (Remember Kellyn's friend from the last chapter?) And she keeps on throwing until that first baby pops out. It typically doesn't take long for said woman to put away her stones. Or if she's a humble sort of gal, she might arrange them in altar fashion and confess her self-righteous attitude.

I can't remember being so bold as to give out parenting advice before I had kids. I do remember *thinking* things like, "My kids are *not* going out in public in clothes that don't match or hair that isn't brushed." (Ha!) Or, "My kids are *not* going to throw fits in the middle of Wal-Mart." (Yesterday was the latest in a rather lengthy run of grocery-store tantrums.) Or, "I will *never* bribe my kids with candy in exchange for promises of good behavior." (Their teeth are rotting as I speak.)

So what do you do when a childless friend, co-worker, relative, or even a mere acquaintance says something offensive to you as a parent when they obviously have no clue what they're talking about? For instance, the newly-married gal who was tired of her job and told me (mother of two under two) that she couldn't wait to start having kids so she could "sit at home and be lazy all day" like me.

You pray for help to bite your tongue. Tell a fellow parent/friend if you must (No, this isn't biblical, but I know I can't stop you!). Then let it go before gossip festers into bitterness. Humbly ask God to deal with this person however He sees fit should a time come when she is blessed with children. Better yet, *pray* for God to bless her. And then just wait.

And try your best not to jump up and down with glee when she eats her words in a great big juicy slice of humble pie.

Who's at the Center?

Ms. Roller Rink *did* have a point, in a twisted sort of way. Marriage and parenthood do not work best when the kids are running the show. When your life is lived on your children's terms, your family will inevitably suffer.

Kids are selfish by nature and don't know how to be any other way, unless they're taught. A world that revolves around them doesn't do them a bit of good—just a whole lot of harm in the long run. We're setting the wrong example for them if our marriage isn't most important.

They need positive mentors, and they desperately need the stability of two parents in love.

Your kids need to know they are not the center of the universe—or the center of your marriage. Your marriage existed before they came along, and it will keep on going after they leave the house. The challenge will be to find creative ways to show them this while reaffirming your great love for them as well.

They need to know that in a happily functioning family, Mom and Dad's relationship comes first. More important than my attention to my children's needs is my attention to their daddy's needs.

It sounds all fine and good, but it sure isn't easy. Kids are a huge responsibility and most definitely put a strain on even the happiest marriages. They take up more actual time than you will ever have for your husband, that's for sure. The point is that you can make him top priority nonetheless.

Take a moment to answer these true/false questions:

1. I frequently say negative things about my husband to my kids.
2. I use my children to nag my husband to get things done.
3. I cuddle more with my kids than I do with my husband.
4. My kids get the best hours of my day. My husband gets what's left.
5. I enjoy life more when my husband is out of town.
6. My kids sleep with my husband and me. If it gets too crowded, he's the one to leave.
7. I rarely, if ever, leave my kids to go out with my husband.
8. I don't ask for his input when it comes to raising the kids.
9. I praise my kids, but not my husband.
10. I think my husband is selfish to ask for sex at the end of a long day.

Obviously, *false* was the answer we were going for here. Did you pass the test?

A Common Mom Problem

As any mom can tell you, deep down we long to be needed by our children. They love and admire us in such a pure and devoted way. We crave that adoration and affection, and it's just not the same coming from our husbands.

If we're not careful, parenting can become a very selfish endeavor for us mommas. I don't always truly want what is best for my daughters. Sometimes I want what is best for *me*. I want them to love and cherish me. I want them to be my friend and like me for always. I need them to need me. They make me feel good about myself.

Of course you should love your kids with all your heart, but finding your *worth* in your children isn't good for you—or for them. It's dangerous and unhealthy to try to meet your emotional emptiness through your kids' love and affection. That burden rests on our heavenly Father, the only one who can truly give us our worth.

We love our children so much and want to be the center of their lives, but we must remember something: Our approach to parenting should always take into consideration the temporary nature of the job. Our quest for meaning and self-worth is not the main point. Our objective should be to raise self-sufficient human beings who can manage life just fine without us. As time goes on, our kids should be taking more responsibility for their own decisions and actions. That's healthy.

Not only is this emotional dependence on your kids unhealthy for you and them, it's bad for your husband as well. It is vitally important that you not send your husband the message that your kids are all you need in order to feel fulfilled.

Your children don't really care if they fulfill you or not. They are egocentric little beings. Your husband, on the other hand, does care about satisfying you. He desperately wants to, in fact.

Hundreds of men have written to Dr. Laura Schlessinger about "their pain of being marginalized after their children were born." Their wives express verbally, or with their actions, that love, affection, or sex with hubby has taken a back seat to motherhood. They only have the time and energy to care for one person—their child. Says Dr. Laura, "This puts fathers in the ugly and uncomfortable position of feeling competitive with and resentful of their children, whom they love so much."

We wear ourselves down taking care of our children and doing everything else we think needs done, and since hubby is "a big boy," he can take care of himself, thank you very much. Or worse, we attack him for his "inconsiderate, unreasonable expectations" like wanting to just enjoy being at home and maybe having sex two or three times a week.

What am I saying to Gabe when I'm willing to get up three or four times a night to nurse a newborn and fill sippy cups with cold water, but I act like 20 minutes of sex would just be the most ridiculous imposition?

My husband needs to come first!

Date/Family Night

One practical way to put him first is to spend time with him alone—no children. Gabe and I have tried (sometimes successfully, sometimes not) to establish a weekly date night. We leave our girls with one of our moms or a trusted friend and get away for awhile.

Don't feel guilty leaving your kids—you're doing them a favor! Lorilee Craker suggests that you as a mom "pry yourself away from your precious progeny from time to time" and spend some quality time with your husband. "If you're one of those people who think you can recapture romance while you're still in the presence of your children," she says, "well, I'll just tell you: you can't!"

In the long run, your kids are not going to resent you for having a date night. They'll secretly be pleased. If, right now, your kids struggle with you and Daddy leaving them one night a week, make it up to them by planning a family night once a week as well.

Play games. Eat your favorite snacks. Watch a movie. Make your own movie. Pop popcorn. Order pizza. Make pizza. Make crafts. Go to the park.

Just make it consistent. And make it special.

"When you have fun as a family, the benefits flow to each family member," David and Claudia Arp say in their book *No Time for Sex*. "Having fun together encourages you to interact and stay in touch with each other's lives. Laughing together diffuses tension and helps you keep short accounts with one another."

When you're making your home fun for your kids, they're going to be more willing to let you go out on a date without them.

Marriage and parenthood should be fun. If you're not enjoying them at this present moment, it's time to rethink things. You don't want to be someone who's always thinking that life will be better somewhere down the road. It rarely ever is.

Spontaneous Sex?

"Sex loses some serious snap, crackle and pop once the kiddies arrive on the scene," Lorilee Craker says. "For many parents, the pitter-patter of little feet is a death knell that tolls for their passionate love life."

Ain't that the truth?

"I am in 'mom mode' all day," Erin says. "Sometimes I feel like I have turned the sexual side of myself off, because I'm a mom."

Couples without children definitely have an advantage when it comes to having sex whenever and wherever they want. Once kids enter the picture, no more making love on the dining room table after a candlelight dinner.

"It limits the time of day we can have sex," Andrea says.

"We're only able to do it at night now," Hannah laments.

"Sex life?" asks Stacey. "What sex life? Now, it's less spontaneous and more guarded."

"We're unable to be spontaneous," says Beth. "Sex is usually in the bedroom only and only at night unless the kids are asleep or at Grandma's house."

"Kids definitely take most of the spontaneity out of sex because you have to do it when they're asleep or take them to a sitter," says Jenna. "When they're home, you have to rush it because you know they will wake up or else you need to get some sleep because they'll be up in several hours."

Okay, we get it. Kids come, and spontaneity takes a flying leap out the window. Then, when they get older, there's the whole "I hope to goodness they don't hear us!" factor.

"You always wonder if you will wake them up being too noisy while in the act!" Jada says.

Kate and her husband are determined to find a solution to this problem. "We are learning to plan it and do it," she says, "despite being tired or worrying that they might hear us."

Lynn and her hubby have come up with a couple plans as well. "Often, we will have sex while my husband is changing from work," she says. "Those may be the quickies, but the kids are none the wiser. Early morning sex (before they're up) also works out well. You have to remember, you are a wife also and you cannot ignore your husband's needs to care for the kids."

A Question of Quantity

One big question parents face is—how many children will we have? I know the Bible says to be fruitful and multiply, but I think there are two keys for determining the number of offspring that is right for your family: 1) Have only as many children as you can handle while still meeting your husband's needs; 2) Don't have more children than your husband wants to have.

What is the magic number? It's going to be different for every woman. For me, that much-prayed-about number is *three*.

I am not condemning women who choose to have large families—not at all. Especially if both the husband and the wife feel God's call on their lives to do so. Some women can handle four or five or more and still keep their husbands happy and fulfilled.

I know one happily married couple with eight children. Their kids are well-behaved and their family life runs quite smoothly. They have an amazing babysitting system set up so that they are able to get away— alone—quite often to spend a relaxing and refreshing time together.

My sister's husband comes from a family of six kids, and I've always been impressed by his mom's ability to raise six well-balanced kids to adulthood all the while keeping her hubby quite satisfied.

Our friends Steve and Cherith don't believe in using birth control.

They feel that God will give them as many children as He wants them to have. Their choice may not be for everyone, but the key is that they are unified in their decision.

Life is not always a breeze for these families, but they are committed to serving God, keeping their marriage strong, and raising their children to love the Lord.

On the other hand, I know another couple with ten children—some biological, some adopted—whose marriage is floundering. The husband, in a desperate attempt to get his sexual needs met somewhere, anywhere,

Wrong Answer, Sister!

I once heard a woman say that she hated the thought of having to go out and get a job once her kids were in school, so her plan was to just keep having to have babies so she'd never get to that point. Not a good reason for having children.

Another woman admitted, "There's nothing I'm really good at. I don't have any remarkable talents. Once I realized how good I was at carrying and delivering babies, I didn't want to stop. This is my talent. When I'm done having babies, where will I find my worth?" Having children to fill a void in your own life—also not good.

I was watching a popular talk show one afternoon. The host was talking to a woman who had two young children and wanted a couple more. Her husband felt that two was plenty and that she had a hard enough time caring for the children they already had.

"But I just love being pregnant, and I love the newborn baby stage," the wife lamented. "I love maternity clothes and nursing and the way babies smell."

When asked if she liked the ages her children were now (five and three), she admitted, "Not really. They're a lot harder to take care of now, and I miss when they were babies."

The talk show host gently—and slightly sarcastically—reminded this woman that any children we choose to have are our sole responsibility for at least 18 years. A child has that "newborn smell" (which I agree is absolutely intoxicating) for about one-fiftieth of that time. Each pregnancy and newborn you enjoy so much quickly turns into a toddler, a kid, a teenager—yours for life.

turned to pornography and is now trapped in Satan's lair. His wife is hurting and angry. Their marriage is crumbling.

Good Sex = Better Daddy

No one wants to hear a woman rave incessantly about her fabulous husband, but I have to for a moment, just to make a point. My husband has three daughters, ages five, three, and six weeks. He cuddles and loves on the baby, showering her with kisses and sweet baby talk. She rewards him with ear-to-ear grins. And he gets down on the floor with the older two, and they eat it up. He plays monster and Prince Charming, hide-and-seek and tag. He builds snowmen and gives sled rides.

He's an awesome dad. It took him a while to find his daddy groove, but once he found it, he took off! And the more I minister to his sexual needs, the more he acts like Daddy of the Year. Conversely, when I ignore his needs, our girls are adversely affected.

There are two ways to go about getting your husband to be a better father. Nag him to spend time with the kids and criticize his parenting shortcomings. Or meet his needs in the bedroom, no strings attached.

Only one way works.

When your husband is sexually satisfied and feels loved completely by his wife, he is able to focus on the kids and give them the kind of love he feels from you.

And it's a two-way street. Watching Gabe interact with our daughters turns me on. And being satisfied sexually is a huge motivator for him to lavish time and affection on his little ladies. It's a beautiful cycle, actually.

It only becomes a vicious one when one of you refuses to do your part. Don't let that person be you.

LET THE GOOD TIMES ROLL!

Chapter 16

Relighting the Fire

What if your marriage is a little stale? What can you do? How about taking a moment to reflect back on those feelings you had when your love was fresh and new?

The flirting you did on the night you first met. The butterflies in your stomach on your first date. The tears of joy you shed when you got engaged. The moment you said "I do" and were overcome with emotion. Your whirlwind honeymoon.

Have you forgotten why you fell in love with your husband in the first place? Maybe it's time to reminisce and rekindle those flames that burned so brightly in the beginning.

❧

It was a stifling Sunday afternoon in June. I pulled into the winding, hilly drive, less than thrilled to be at Scioto Hills Baptist Camp, my new home for the next two months. I had left my "significant other" at college the day before, packed up my whole life in a single day, and missed my cousin's wedding all to be a camp counselor. I knew I was following God's call, but I was still depressed.

After unloading my luggage into my cabin, I wandered over to the basketball court where two guys were playing one-on-one. They politely stopped their game to introduce themselves. I beat them to the punch.

"Hi there. I'm Marla." I wasn't prepared for what came next.

"Marla Yoder, right?" the younger one asked.

"Yeah…" I answered, less confident than before. "And you are…?"

"I'm Tug," he answered with a grin. "I'm dating your cousin."

The light came on. "Oh! I've heard a lot about you!"

"And I'm Gabe, his brother," the older one said.

"Nice to meet you both. Care if I play?" I asked.

Whether they cared or not, I don't know. But they let me play. And they showed me no mercy. Gabe blocked my shot eight times in ten minutes.

I don't believe in love at first sight, but the attraction was undeniable. And I spent most of the summer trying to deny it! But by the time summer gave way to the falling leaves of autumn, I knew I wanted to marry this guy.

Well, you may be saying, I'm glad you and your husband fell in love at first sight and all, but our story isn't so great. We met at a bar—we were drunk. Or, I have no idea when we first met. I've known him all my life. Or, he was dating my best friend and cheated on her with me.

Though you may not have a magical story to tell, I'll bet you can see God's hand in it if you look closely enough. Think about it and pray about it. He's the One who can bring good out of not-so-good.

Real-Life Cinderellas

Do you have vivid recollections of your engagement day? Or has the memory gone fuzzy over time? I asked several women to share memorable moments from their husbands' proposals. Some of them were simple, some elaborate, some funny, some boring. One woman said, "We argue about who proposed to whom!"

Another woman, who had been married 16 years, commented, "I can't remember. That's kinda sad." Yes, it is. No matter how or when or where you got engaged, you should write down your experience and tuck a memory or two away in your heart for life.

If you're disappointed because your husband's proposal wasn't the enchanted evening under the stars you'd always dreamed about, don't worry! Years from now, it's not going to matter, and maybe you'll be able to laugh together about it.

Many women shared tidbits with me of their engagement stories, ones that lacked romance—no chocolates, candlelight dinners, roses, or dancing—but were memorable nonetheless.

"He proposed to me in the church parking lot in the most horrible old yellow and black Vega car. How I want to forget that car!"

"I went to the doctor and found out I was going to have a baby. We went straight to the jewelers from the doctor's office, picked out our rings, and got married five months later. I was so scared."

"We were sitting at the reservoir four days after our first date, and Jon said to me he didn't want to date anyone else ever again. We got engaged about six weeks later."

"We went to a golfing range and hit golf balls. I bumped into him and felt a small box in his pocket but wasn't thinking. When he took me home, we sat on my front porch, and he asked me to marry him. I hesitated. He said if I didn't marry him now, I never would, so I said yes."

"It wasn't very dramatic. He won a trip to Rio de Janeiro and wanted it to be our honeymoon. We both knew we were right for each other, and he asked me to marry him."

"I was at his house getting ready to get together with friends. I went upstairs to find him, and he came around the corner on his knees and proposed."

"We went to get the ring between my high school baseball team's doubleheader. We made it back in time for the second game."

"We went to a special restaurant and sat by a fireplace. Before that, he had gone to talk to my parents and said, 'I knew everything would be okay because your mom made me pie.'"

"There was no pre-engagement or talk of a wedding or marriage. He asked me to marry him, and I said yes."

"I thought he was joking because we'd only been face-to-face three times prior to him asking (we did write letters in between)."

Be a Realistic Romantic

I hope to give you some practical ideas for bringing back a slew of wonderful memories, but let me offer a quick word of warning first. In general, we women are more sentimental, emotional, and romantic-minded than men. If your husband balks at the idea of spending a "boring" evening in front of the fireplace reminiscing about the past, make it a more exciting activity.

Go out one evening and do something he really enjoys. Let him pick his favorite restaurant and favorite activity (putt-putt, bowling, hiking—anything but a movie). Start reminiscing "on the sly"—just a little bit at a time. A brief comment here and there. "Hey, do you remember that time we…?" or "Wasn't it funny when we both…" or "Tell me again when you first found yourself liking me as more than a friend…"

Don't force him to share his feelings or to answer deep and thought-provoking questions. Just take it nice and easy. And remember—meeting *his* needs first (like sex in particular) will help him be more open to reflecting on the past with you in a way you find romantic.

Engaging Your Senses

Have you ever thought about your sense of smell and the memories it can evoke? Try this: Right before you take the sheets off your bed to wash them, take a whiff of your pillow and then your husband's. It's amazing how different they smell.

Just the other day, we visited Gabe's parents at their log cabin. As I walked in the door, I took a deep breath and instantly got goose bumps. I felt like I had been transported back to our dating days. Eight years later, the smell of amazing memories almost knocked me off my feet.

Find a smell that reminds you of your dating days or when you were first married. Maybe there's a place you could visit that has a distinct smell—a park, a field, someone's home, a college dorm. Maybe it's Chapstick you wore, shampoo you used, cologne he wore, the kind of detergent he used, or the gum you always chewed.

I've kept a tiny jar of potpourri from our first apartment. Every time I open it, memories of our early days come flooding back. I'll never part with that bottle!

Senses can affect our love lives in a powerful way. "Our five physical senses provide one of the keys that unlock and influence our emotions," Karen Linamen points out. We all have "sensory triggers" that are linked to past experiences, both positive and negative.

Think of some other sensory experiences that trigger pleasurable emotions in you and your husband. The key is to harness some of those smells, tastes, textures, sounds, and sights and use them to your advantage during lovemaking.

Just be careful which sensory triggers you choose…

Name that Smell

"Who pooped?" my husband wanted to know as he walked in the front door the other day kicking snow off his boots.

"What do you mean, who *pooped?*" I asked. "Do you *smell* poop?"

"No, but I smell *matches*," was his reply.

I had to chuckle. I had just lit a Christmas candle to fill our home with delicious scents of the season, and Gabe's first thought was, "Someone stunk up the bathroom and had to light a match."

The fact of the matter is, we associate smells with things. With people, with places, with events. Gabe just happened to have a certain association that went along with the smell of matches.

Why not pick a special fragrance that you associate with sex (like vanilla candles)? Or find a special perfume for you and cologne for him. Splash some on only when you're together and the opportunity for sex is in your immediate future.

Adding a second sense will help fortify the experience in your mind. Choose a song or CD that you play softly while you make love. Then each time you smell vanilla or hear, "Have You Ever Loved a Woman?" you'll be reminded of the act of making love to your husband.

Tommy Nelson says that men love to employ all of their senses while making love. He shares these senses in the order of what he says excites men most: What he hears during sex, what he sees, what he feels, what he smells, what he tastes. He encourages wives to use the "whole arsenal at your disposal!"

God gave us five senses to use and enjoy. By learning to engage our senses throughout the day, we'll be better prepared to use them at night in bed with our husbands.

One of the best places to practice using your senses is in the great outdoors—in God's beautiful creation. I urge you to read through the Song of Songs and pick out all the references to fruits and flowers, gardens and vineyards. Here's an example: "While the king was at his table, my perfume spread its fragrance. My lover is to me a sachet of myrrh resting between my breasts. My lover is to me a cluster of henna blossoms from the vineyards of En Gedi."

These lovers inhaled God's goodness with all of their senses, and it translated into a burning arousal for each other.

Bring Back Those Memories

What are you going to do to rekindle the flames? What can you do to bring back the memories of romantic times gone by?

Here are some good memory triggers: Ask friends and family to send you copies of photos they might have taken of the two of you that you've never seen or have forgotten about. Or ask them to share memories of the two of you from the very beginning—they may remember things you've long since forgotten.

My sister Bethany made a memorable gift for her husband, Stewart, when they got married. She looked back through old journals from her younger days and clipped out all the parts where she talked about her hopes and dreams for her future husband. She glued hundreds of snippets into a new journal and presented it to Stewart as they began their life together.

You could also make a scrapbook of your dating days, if you saved any memorabilia such as restaurant napkins, snapshots, maps from zoos or amusement parks, gift tags, short love notes, receipts, and so on. If, like me, scrapbooking isn't your thing, gather up anything you've saved and put it in a special photo box or plastic storage box and label it as your "Precious Memories."

If you kept a journal when you first met or while you were dating or engaged, read back through it and share tender (or funny) passages

What a Day!

Four months after we were married, Gabe and I pulled out our wedding video for the first time. As I watched, I marveled at how God orchestrated the whole day to bring glory to Himself—in spite of us.

Family played a huge part in our special day. Our siblings made beautiful bridesmaids and handsome groomsmen. Our two-year-old cousins acted at least twice their age as ringbearer and flower girl. And my aunt and uncle sang the special music—all our favorite praise songs.

We surprised my dad with a video Gabe made. Right after Dad walked me down the aisle, a big screen came down and one of his favorite songs, "Butterfly Kisses," began to play as pictures of a little Marla and her daddy showed up on the screen. For the second time in my life, I saw my Dad cry.

After we had exchanged vows and rings, Gabe gave a neat talk about families and shared the gospel, as we had many unsaved family members in attendance.

After Gabe carried me out of the sanctuary like a potato sack, the wedding party sat in the front row to watch another video Gabe had made. Little Marla dressed as an Indian. Then little Indian Gabe. Little Marla in shades. Little Gabe in shades. Marla in her birthday suit. Gabe in his. It was a big hit with the crowd.

The reception flew by so fast I barely remember it. I do remember my brother Josh delighting the audience with a juggling act set to music. I remember Gabe tossing the garter over his head, taped to a soccer ball! I remember eating about two bites of food and thinking, Is this all really happening to me?

As we drove off to our honeymoon with birdseed caked in our hair and two-liter bottles dragging behind us, we thanked God for His incredible goodness!

with your husband. Go for a walk, and think of as many things as you can that you did on your dates before you got married. Share with each other what your first impressions were of your mate.

Even if you hate to write, make yourself write things down that happen(ed) early in your marriage. You won't remember them clearly if you don't. And reminiscing about special times, good or bad, can enrich your marriage in a way that can't be duplicated. You can always create new memories, but you can never re-create the old ones if you've forgotten them.

Your stories don't have to be anything spectacular. Most of us don't live lives thrilling enough to be made into a movie. But remembering fun, interesting, hilarious, or frightening times you've shared can be rewarding.

One thing I've found helpful is taking ten seconds (or less) a day to jot a phrase or two on my desk calendar about what we did that day. If it weren't for those little phrases, I wouldn't be able to look back at a month and tell you more than one or two things that happened. But just looking at that one little phrase works wonders at triggering my memory.

Keep it simple. *Went to Chili's—chicken fajitas. Fell while rollerblading. Watched* Top Gun *(forty-fourth time). Tried new restaurant—Gino's—hated it. Played tennis—won first game ever. Ran out of gas on I-75. Raccoon knocked over our garbage—huge mess. Visited Grandma in nursing home— she remembered us. Put oven mitt on burner—oops! New mower—love it. Made stromboli together—yum.*

Sometimes it's the little things that make the most special memories.

Did you ever write love letters to each other or a list of "50 Reasons Why I Love You"? Do it again. Did you ever take walks, holding hands the entire way? Do it again. Did you used to surprise each other with small (sometimes homemade) gifts? Do it again. Did you ever make a CD or MP3 of love songs for your love? Do it again.

If you kissed for hours when you were dating, and now ten seconds seems like an eternity, time to get back into make-out mode. Start by kissing for thirty seconds. The next time, do it for a minute. Then five. Start making time for long make-out sessions. They might lead somewhere else; they might not. But hopefully, they'll remind you of those days when just kissing your man was an absolute delight.

Partners, Not Roommates

Do you and your husband still *play* together like you did when you were dating? What were some of your favorite activities? Rollerblading? Miniature golf? Bowling? How about riding bikes? Midnight Wal-Mart runs? Art museums? Baseball games?

"We have all known couples who seem to go their separate ways even though they are still technically married," author Tommy Nelson says. "He does his thing, she does her thing, and the two of them rarely do the same thing."

Do you know a couple like that? Are *you* one-half of a couple like that?

"That is not faithful commitment," Tommy says. "Marriage calls a person to a oneness of identity with another person."

He's not saying that you have to give up all of your interests just to do what your hubby likes to do. And hubby doesn't need to do that for *you* either. But Tommy feels, and I agree, that it's important to find things you can enjoy together. It's okay to have alone time, or girlfriend time, but the majority of your activities should take place *with* your spouse, not *without* him. You're life *partners,* not just roommates.

Like we talked about before, making time for your hubby often means sacrificing some of your own personal time. Yes, there are times we need to regroup, re-gather, and refresh ourselves…alone. But "*hubby* time" should trump "*me* time" *every* time.

Lots of guys would love for their wives to take an interest in, and get involved in, their hobbies. Ask your husband how he feels about this. If he wants to hunt alone, don't pester him. But if he'd love for you to learn to golf, go for it!

Pray about finding an activity you can do together that you really enjoy. If he has something in mind that doesn't appeal to you, pray that God will open your heart and mind to the good in it and help you find it enjoyable. Who knows? Sometimes when you just give things a chance, they can really grow on you.

We can't live in the past, of course, but your history with your spouse can give hope and meaning and purpose to the present and your future together. When your marriage seems humdrum, stale, shaky, or even troubled, sometimes a glance back into your past together can breathe new life into your relationship with your husband today. Karen Linamen suggests, "Let yesterday's memories cast their golden glow on your attitudes today." Here's to golden, glowing attitudes!

Pulling the Wool over My Eyes

You thought you weren't going to hear the rest of my engagement story, right? Well, I can't resist telling you more about what happened after that day on the basketball court.

It was a sweltering Saturday morning in July. Gabe and I were back at church camp for our second summer together. Our relationship had progressed quickly. He already had my ring. I had picked it out myself, so I wasn't expecting his proposal to be much of a surprise.

The last camper had gone home. It was time for our afternoon staff meeting, and then freedom until Sunday evening. I couldn't wait.

I should have been suspicious that morning, but I wasn't. Every other day that summer, butterflies made nests in my stomach lining as I wondered if Gabe would pop the question. But that day, it never really crossed my mind. God must have shut my brain, like he did the lions' mouths for Daniel.

For starters, the camp director asked Gabe to lead everyone in singing "This Is the Day" at breakfast. That was a neon sign if there ever was one. Gabe would rather clean toilets than sing in front of people.

My parents and Gabe's were both at camp that morning to pick up campers—their first time there together.

I stood talking to my brother for 15 minutes while Gabe sat at a table 20 feet behind me asking my dad if he could marry me. I never turned around once!

My dad hugged me over and over that morning, each time squeezing the breath out of me, saying, "Are you my girl?" Uh, yeah...sure, Dad. Why wouldn't I be?

Nearly 30 people knew Gabe's plan, and not one of them let it slip!

We pulled out of the driveway after our staff meeting and headed toward the mall. Gabe informed me that the camp director had asked him to pick up a film projector on our way. A local pastor was donating it to the camp.

"It shouldn't take long," he assured me, "and then we'll have the rest of the day to ourselves."

Twenty minutes later, we pulled into the pastor's driveway. The house was on a bank overlooking the Ohio River. I breathed in the smell of freshly mowed grass and flowers in full bloom and commented on the beauty of our surroundings. The entire landscape was spring green. The river flowed peacefully by, the sun's rays bouncing off the tiny waves in all directions.

I got out of the car and walked to the edge of the embankment to get a better view. There were steps leading down to the water's edge, and a small clearing in a grove of trees. I gasped when I noticed a small table with a white lace table-cloth and two chairs. On the table were candles, place settings for two, and my favorite—white roses!

"Oh, look!" I said. "Isn't that *nice!* That pastor must be *so* sweet—setting up this romantic little dinner for his wife!"

I knew my practical, no-nonsense boyfriend wouldn't give two hoots about some mushy pastor, so I turned away and headed for the house. Gabe grabbed my hand and said, "Let's come down here for a minute."

All I could think was, *Oh, we can't! What if the pastor and his wife* catch *us? How embarrassing!* (Yes, I'm an idiot.)

He took my hand and led me to the steps. We were halfway down when I *finally* realized what was going on.

"Oh my goodness." I said, dumbfounded. "Oh my goodness!" I wrapped him in a huge hug and began to cry.

He somehow wriggled free from my suffocating embrace, got down on one knee, and pulled a ring box from his pocket. "Will you marry me?" he asked, and then tacked on a "please?" for good measure. He later told me he said "please" four times before I finally answered. I didn't even hear him!

Then he led me to the table and pulled out my chair. Tied around each of the 12 white roses was a note or verse. He reached under the table with a grin and pulled out a pizza and breadsticks! I squealed in delight when I saw half of the pepperoni pizza adorned with black olives (*his* favorite) and half with green olives (*my* favorite).

Sigh.

Chapter 17

Sugar and Spice

want to do something different tonight," I told Gabe the other night. "I'm tired of the same-ol'-same-ol'." We had scheduled a lovemaking date for 11:00. The hour came, and I was bummed.

His eyes lit up, and he hit the ball back in my court. "You're the one writing the sex book and doing all the research," he reminded me. "What new thing do you want to try?"

I had a sinking feeling this was going to end in a fight. I hadn't communicated my feelings very well. I wasn't looking for a new *position*.

What I had *really* meant was, "I want us to connect first *emotionally*. I want to *feel* intimate with you before we ever get to the bedroom, so sex won't feel so cold and lifeless and matter-of-fact."

When it comes to a fulfilling sex life, I'm a firm believer that intimacy trumps variety. Variety may very well be the spice of life, but is not the end-all answer to troubles in your sex life. It's definitely no substitute for unselfishness. Mixing it up to stave off boredom is great and all, but your ultimate pursuit should be of *intimacy,* not the latest, greatest sexual idea.

Fun should not be the primary goal of sex—it is not the greatest good that comes from it. If fun is your only goal, you'll get bored quickly, and dissatisfaction will characterize your sex life.

However, variety ain't a bad idea—and it can actually lead to greater intimacy. Variety and creativity can greatly enhance a loving, giving, sexual relationship. When your husband realizes the time and effort you put into finding new ways to love him physically, it will do nothing but bring you closer emotionally.

In *Red-Hot Monogamy*, Bill and Pam Farrel say, "In a marriage, sex

Spicy Hot

Can the marriage bed get too spicy? My friend Rayna would submit that it is quite possible. She recently shared a humorous story of a sexual encounter where her husband really turned up the heat.

Cal and Rayna had just returned home from a New Year's Eve party at Cal's office. What better way to ring in the New Year than to make some love, Cal thought. And Rayna agreed.

They were both in an amorous mood, and Rayna couldn't wait for Cal to start touching her. As he made her way down her body, Rayna shivered with delight. Then giggled with glee. Then screamed in pain.

Hand pressed between her legs, she sprinted to the bathroom. The burning sensation in her most private of parts was almost unbearable—and utterly inexplicable.

Well, not quite. Turns out there was a logical explanation after all. You see, good ol' Cal was known throughout the office for his tantalizing, spicy-hot homemade salsa. Upon request, he had churned out a big batch for the party earlier that day.

He thought he had thoroughly washed the jalapeno juice off his hands. Maybe, though, he'd gotten sidetracked while taste-testing his exquisite concoction. Who knows?

All Rayna knew was that it had better never happen again.

"Yeah, when working with hot peppers, wash your hands really good before you make love," a repentant Cal advises fellow husbands.

"It's me or the salsa, Cal," laughs Rayna.

It's okay to spice up your love life—just don't do it literally.

is the spice that rescues our relationships from becoming mundane pursuits of chores."

If you and your husband have gotten into a lovemaking rut and want to spice things up, this chapter is for you! You owe it to yourself to fully enjoy the sexual side of life.

Keep Him Coming Back

In all seriousness, we live in a day and age of high stimulation and low attention spans. We get bored easily. We're always looking for something new and exciting to keep us entertained.

Every sexual experience doesn't have to involve something brand spankin' new. That's impossible. But your love life can be reinvigorated if you make an effort to infuse it with some creativity.

Some women want to know why their husbands don't want to spend more time at home with them. Maybe we're the ones to blame. What are we doing to make our homes exciting places to be? Who says we should have to leave the house to find a thrill?

Kevin Leman says that men are either home-centered or outside-the-home-centered. "If a man is home-centered," he says, "it's likely because the queen is keeping the king pretty happy!" He goes on to say that if a man is centered on something other than home, he'll always have to leave home to recharge his batteries.

Are we pursuing our husbands in a sexual way? Does he come home at night with the assurance that he'll be gettin' some good lovin'? Does he look forward to the new and exciting twist he knows you'll be putting on your time together? Does he rush home to you when he wants his batteries recharged? Does his thrill-seeking radar consistently point him to *you*?

Creative sex takes time and effort, and the fact that you put effort into making sex exciting will please your husband like nothing else.

Study your husband's body. Learn and remember what excites him. You don't serve the same meal for supper every night. Don't serve up the same "sex recipe" every time either. The missionary position can be fabulous—but not if you're using it every single time you make love. Mix it up, girl! Get spicy!

I'm not going to give you a list of 50 wild new sexual positions. All but four or five of them would be uncomfortable—if not painful—anyway. Sex should feel *good*. And sex is much more than which way you line up your bodies on any given night.

I am typically content to stick with tried-and-true positions with "if it ain't broke, don't fix it" as my mantra. Gabe has asked me on a number of occasions, "Wanna try something new tonight?" and I usually answer, "Maybe next time."

Lately, I've tried to take him up on his offer and change things up a bit. We still have our "familiar favorites," but there's something to be said for variety as well. You'll never know unless you try!

"A marriage that cools and grows stale is not biblical!" declares Tommy Nelson. "It is worldly wisdom that makes it acceptable. Rebel against such error!"

Creative Juices

Here are a few ideas just to get you started. Some I've tried, some I plan to try soon. Some are simple, some a little more involved. Some take quite a bit of planning and effort. I encourage you to take some of these creative ideas to heart—and to bed!

- First of all—new lingerie. You don't have to spend a ton on it, but if you have some extra money, here is a good place to splurge. Ask your husband what he likes—lace, see-through, leather, black, bright colors, animal prints. A new negligee says to your hubby, "I put some thought into pleasing you ahead of time."
- Change up the lighting and music. Different color lightbulbs—black, red, and purple are fun. Lots of candles. One candle. A sexy CD.
- Try covering your bed with a plastic sheet or shower curtain and your bodies with baby oil, and let the wild and crazy fun begin! If you're like me and hate the thought of such a slimy mess—get over it! I'm determined to try this in the next month.
- Play strip poker. Or strip foosball. Or air hockey. Or Scrabble. Or Go Fish. Or Ping-Pong. Make up your own rules. Just make sure you get naked.
- Make love in a sleeping bag. Outside in the yard if it's secluded.
- Ask your husband what one of his sexual fantasies is. Then fulfill it.

- Go skinny-dipping. And make love in the pool.
- Develop a code word or phrase for sex that you can use when you're in a crowd. For example, "We need to have a conference" or "Mr. Jones would like to see you now."
- When you're on your way home from somewhere, slide your hand up your husband's shorts or down his pants. Or caress him through his clothes. See how fast he runs into the house when you get home (if you make it there)!
- Before you walk into a restaurant, tell your husband you're not wearing any panties. (I *must* try this one this year!)
- Put on old clothes and go play in the mud. Then make love in the shower—before, after, or while you're washing off. It's up to you!
- Place erotic notes in strategic places throughout the day (where no one will see them but your husband!) leading up to a passionate night of making love.
- *Red-Hot Monogamy,* by Bill and Pam Farrel, is a great idea book for married couples. It's a great read, with 200 ideas for livening up your relationship.

"At our door is every delicacy, both new and old," Solomon's lover tells him in the Song of Songs, "that I have stored up for you, my lover." Are we storing up sexual delicacies for our husbands?

We wives can always be more creative in our lovemaking. Be imaginative, resourceful, innovative! Make it your goal to always be thinking up new treats for your hubby. As an example, last December, I planned to use some of my Christmas money on some new lingerie. I asked Gabe what colors and styles he liked. Then I found three cute little numbers on sale for $1.97 each—just like Gabe had requested. The Lord provides!

Now, *reading* about these ideas won't do a lick of good. You need to do one of them—in the next three days. Are they a bit out of your comfort zone? Good! That is precisely the point! A life lived within the confines of a comfort zone is b-o-r-i-n-g.

Make Your Home a Sexual Haven

I have grand dreams for that "someday" when I will have enough time, money, and resources to turn my home into somewhat of a resort for my husband and me. The huge master bedroom with a king-sized bed and attached master bath. The spacious garden tub with picture windows and a to-die-for view. The hot tub on the screened-in back porch. The gazebo and waterfalls in our backyard. The two-person hammock hanging between two giant oak trees. A restful, relaxing, sexually inviting paradise.

Once I have all that, I'll want to have sex all the time.

The problem with right now is my three preschool daughters, my 1500-square-foot house, neighbors on every side, no deck, no hot tub, no master bathroom, a small and boring bedroom with a small and boring bed, neglected landscaping...

But once I move into my dream home...

Here's the trouble. If we can't work with what we've got and make sex a fun, exciting part of our marriages, we won't ever be able to do it. Not even with a hot tub and a hammock. We've got to learn to quit yearning for something that could be years down the road and make do with what we have today.

If we don't, this is what will happen. In ten years, we might have the dream home on the gorgeous property with every amenity known to man, but our marriage will be in the pits. So far gone that it's unsalvageable. And then what good will all our stuff do us?

Yes, money can help enhance your sex life. But at the core of a good sexual relationship with your husband is your attitude and the effort you put into it. It has nothing to do with what you can and can't afford.

Go ahead and dream big. Dream together. But in the meantime, in the here and now, make sex a priority.

So your bathtub isn't a Jacuzzi. Make love in it anyway. If you've got kids, be sure to clear out the goggles and plastic starfish first!

So your bedroom is tiny. Fill it with candles and a bouquet of fresh flowers (a big aphrodisiac) and a CD of sensual music.

So you don't have a gazebo or a hammock. Take some couch cushions, blankets, and kitchen chairs and make a fort—what a fun place for sex!

Make the most of what you've been given!

I asked some of my friends to share what they've done with their bathroom, bedroom, or other areas of their home to make them more romantic.

"A lock!" Wendy said with a laugh. "We keep it minimal with lots of natural light. Our TV has Sirius music on it, so we pick from a nice selection of mood music."

"Vanilla candles," Daphne said. "Yum. We also bought a lamp that gives dim lighting and turn on the AC (so we don't get sweaty and so the neighbors can't hear us)."

"When we chose a plan for our home we had a getaway in mind," Jodie told me, "and that is what we got. Our room is on the main floor. It is large with huge windows and a beautiful view of the woods (and birds). We also have a large bath and Jacuzzi. Joanna's room is upstairs, and it makes it so nice, because when I put my precious baby to bed, we never have to worry about waking her up or anything. We have a lock on our bedroom door for the future, of course (when Joanna grows up into a snooper)."

Sex as a Hobby

Imagine what life would be like if sex were one of your favorite hobbies. Think of your favorite things to do now—something you invest time, money, and energy in. For many women (myself excluded), it's scrapbooking. They shop Hobby Lobby, Target, Michael's, and Jo Ann Fabrics for the best deals and the hottest new items.

If we like to shop more than we like to have sex, what does that say to our husbands? What if we made *sex* our number-one hobby? What if we scoured TJ Maxx, Target, and the mall looking for ideas to romanticize our bedrooms, embellish our bodies, and enhance our sex lives?

Pick a sexy new color to paint your bedroom. Buy silk sheets and matching candles. Play with the lighting—get a dimmer light. We women need an atmosphere and a mood. That invites the best sex for us.

"I can't afford all that," you say.

I beg to differ. What are you buying right now for just yourself? Make the sacrifice. Just because I don't scrapbook, that doesn't mean I don't spend money on things I don't "need." I love picture frames, stickers, books, magazines, organizational containers, and thank-you notes. What could I give up, so I could purchase something to enhance my sex life and show my husband he matters to me?

If money is really tight, eat macaroni and cheese or tomato soup a night or two a week and use your extra cash to shop for sex.

Making Out Is What You Make It

My first year as a teacher, I was blessed to teach a class of fifth- and sixth-grade gifted and talented students. A typical characteristic of smart kids is that they get bored easily.

As we opened our world history textbook and began reading about ancient civilizations, I had a choice to make. Plod and plow through one lesson after another, reading the text and asking questions, while my brilliant students fought sleep. *Or* I could make history come alive!

We hustled through the first couple chapters of the book and then spent an entire month on ancient Egypt. The kids learned hieroglyphics, fashioned authentic costumes, crafted ancient Egyptian board games, memorized the names of countless gods and goddesses, re-created Tut's tomb, experimented with Egyptian recipes, and put on a program for their parents, the rest of the school, even the school board. We did the same thing with ancient Greece and medieval Europe.

The kids were on fire with excitement—and I got completely caught up in it, too. Their positive attitudes were contagious. History had never been so much fun!

Sex, like the study of ancient history, is what you make it. Teaching in a hands-on way cost me hundreds of extra hours of prep time (like mummy-wrapping baby dolls with toilet paper and tape and spray painting them gold), but it was worth it. Seven years later, the kids remember it all vividly.

A good sex life doesn't come without a price tag—not dollars, but minutes and hours. You'll do well to cough up the extra "dough."

Be the Initiator

Many women think it is the man's job to initiate sex. His biblical duty even. I respectfully disagree.

"Awake, north wind, and come, south wind!" Solomon's wife shouts in the Song of Songs. "Blow on my garden that its fragrance may spread abroad. Let my lover come into his garden and taste its choice fruits."

I'm not sure what all she is proposing to her husband, but I know this much—she's the one unabashedly extending the invitation for sex.

The best sex often takes place when the wife takes the initiative to get the love-fires burning. You've probably found it to be true that when you're turned on, that turns on your hubby. But when *he's* turned on, you feel pressured more than anything. Pressure to give up and give in when it's apparent he's not going to let up.

I don't know about your husband, but Gabe rarely turns down my sexual advances. Only when he's really tired. Find special ways to communicate when you're in the mood. Develop some sort of code for wanting sex. Imagine what that will do to your husband when he sees you flashing "the code."

I once read about a woman named Karen. She and her husband each kept a candle on their side of the bed. When one of them was in the mood, they'd merely light their candle as a signal to their mate. But I had to laugh at Karen's solution for those "headache" nights: "When I'm really *not* in the mood," she says, "I hide all the matches!"

Write sex down in your day-planner. I know—sounds so romantic, right? Scheduling sex doesn't have to be cold and impersonal. Oftentimes, when you plan for sex, you look forward to your time together with great anticipation. Scheduling can actually add excitement to your marriage, because it causes you to think of sex with greater frequency.

Of course, you don't have to limit lovemaking to your desk calendar—do it spontaneously as well.

The afternoon is a really great time to have sex, if you can get an afternoon together alone. Instead of waiting until the end of the day, when one or both of you is exhausted, take a little tryst beneath the sheets by the light of the sun. I think you'll be pleasantly surprised at how much fun it can be.

We find it much easier to do *other* things than sex for our husbands when it comes to expressing love. Things like keeping the house clean, fixing meals, doing laundry, maybe even a back scratch. The thing is, we can multitask while we're serving our husbands in those ways—get other "important" things done at the same time. You know, like talk on the phone, put Band-Aids on our kids' hurt fingers, daydream about the new living-room furniture we want.

It costs a lot for us to make love to our husbands while being completely in the moment. But participating fully—with your mind, heart, and body—will bless your husband in ways you can't imagine.

The Overachieving Lover

In his book *Sacred Sex,* Dr. Tim Gardner includes a section from his wife, Amy, on how fatigue can destroy our sex lives. If this is the case, we're attempting to do too much.

Amy admits that she's guilty of "overfunctioning"—giving 110 percent to hospitality efforts, gift-giving, her latest project. But then she asks herself, "How often have I overfunctioned when planning a sexual encounter with Tim? Not all that often."

"We do difficult things every day," she points out. "Why should we shy away from applying ourselves to mastering the art of holy sex?"

We're overachievers, superwomen—the more we do, the more value we think our lives have. I think it's time to re-align our thinking patterns. Going through life at a hundred miles an hour, being all things to all people at all times—it's not as noble and desirable a life as we've led ourselves to believe.

Why not slow down, relax, and save some of our drive to outdo ourselves in the bedroom? What would your husband say if you prepared a sexual encounter that obviously involved going above and beyond "the call of duty"?

There are a lot of things I've done with my time that I've later regretted. I have never regretted spending time with my husband, cultivating our relationship. The return on my investment is incalculable.

How Important Is Sex?

I was surprised to read the comments of a handful of women who didn't think sex was a top priority in a successful marriage.

"I am blessed to have a happy marriage despite our not being able to find time for sex," one woman said. "Marriage is so much more than the physical. Sex is just the cherry on the sundae of our full life together."

"Sex is a wonderful but small part of our marriage," said another.

"People make sex too big of a deal," said one woman. "It doesn't have to play such a huge role in marriage."

"There are a million other things in a marriage that are more important than sex," one woman said.

My opinion is that these women don't recognize the importance of sex because they're separating emotional love from the physical expression of that love.

I recently read a book by a woman whose husband's health problems put a halt to their sex life. As they found ways to be intimate without intercourse, she was disturbed to read so many books that suggested that sex is the glue that holds marriages together. She strongly disagreed and pointed out that she and her husband were held together by prayer more than anything else.

Her point is certainly valid. When sex is not an option for medical reasons, I truly believe God provides couples with alternative routes to intimacy. And I would never argue against prayer as an intimacy-maker.

However, if you and your husband are both physically able to engage regularly in sex, I absolutely believe it will bond you together like nothing else can. It is the ultimate act of giving yourself wholly and completely to your husband. It will bring you closer than you ever dreamed possible.

"Sex is more than mere skin on skin," as *The Message* paraphrases Paul's words in 1 Corinthians. "Sex is as much spiritual mystery as physical fact."

As Dr. Leman says, "A good sex life colors the marriage from top to bottom."

Intimacy—loving and knowing your spouse completely and being loved and known completely by him—is the ultimate goal of marriage. You want to be more than husband and wife; you want to be soul mates.

God created sex to bring us to that kind of intimacy. With intimacy as our ultimate goal, let's be creative and inventive lovers, making our marriage bed an exciting, fulfilling place to be!

Chapter 18

The Bottom Line

'm not big on workbooks—the kind that come with a lot of wonderful Christian books. I'd rather just sit back, enjoy a book, and not have to worry about answering questions or applying what I've learned. Okay, so maybe it's not so much workbooks I don't like, but *work*. There. I've admitted that I can be rather lazy.

You have just about reached the end of this book. After you have turned the last page, you will have to put the book down and either a) forget about it forever, or b) purpose to put its principles into practice with your partner.

If you are so brave as to choose option b, I won't lie to you—it won't be a piece of cake. But the results can be oh-so-sweet!

The Scenic Route

When I was growing up, our family of six took yearly trips through the mountains of Virginia and North Carolina to visit relatives. It used to drive me nuts when Dad would opt for the "scenic route" instead of the faster, more efficient superhighway. It wasn't until I became an adult that I realized the significance of the scenic route.

Destinations are important, but so are journeys. And we spend more time on the journey anyway. Why not choose the journey that will bring you the most joy?

There are no shortcuts to sweeter sex. It's human nature to look for a faster, easier way to reach our goals. But deep down, if we truly knew what was best for us, a shortcut would never be the answer. With the things that matter most in life, there simply are no shortcuts. Period.

Sometimes, taking the shortcut means cheating yourself out of life's most beautiful (scenic, if you will) moments.

Along those same lines, as I pulled weeds in my backyard this morning, I mopped sweat from my brow with my dirty forearm and thought, "If only I had the money to hire a gardener."

But then I thought twice. Sure, it would save me a lot of work, and my yard would look just as good, if not better. But when I sit in my lounge chair, sipping lemonade in the shade, I'd be admiring someone else's masterpiece, not my own. I could still enjoy the beautiful landscape, but that feeling of utter satisfaction and meaningful exhaustion would be strikingly absent.

When you work for weeks or months on a drawing (or a magazine article, a scrapbook, tiling your kitchen backsplash, painting your living room), how do you feel when the project is finished?

Aaahhh...I did it! My hard work paid off. And now I realize that it was worth every minute. Everything in life that is fulfilling, rewarding, and satisfying is something we worked our tails off for.

This is how we need to look at sex. Forget the easy way out, the shortcut. The more we put into it, the more fulfilling the final outcome will be.

Give It a Go!

My prayer is that you know by now that I didn't write this book to get my kicks, or because I know sex sells.

Rather, I really want to see marriages improve and young wives be encouraged. I know what a huge part sex plays in a good marriage, and what a huge obstacle it is for so many couples—Gabe and I not excluded. A smoothly operating sex life is such a *huge* blessing, and I want women (myself included) to experience it. When you and your husband find fulfillment in bed, *everybody* wins! You, your hubby, your kids, your co-workers, your friends, your ministry partners.

You want to feel emotionally loved and romanced. Your husband wants to feel sexually satisfied and know he's satisfying you. How are you both going to get your needs met?

Here's my advice—you go first! Don't leave it up to him. Give your husband what he needs and, chances are, what you want will follow. But don't wait for everything to get fixed before you meet your husband's physical needs. It will never happen.

The more energy you invest in your sex life, the more energy you'll have. Feelings don't have to come first. Act first, and feelings will follow closely behind.

We often lack the energy and desire—even confidence—for sex. But sex actually *creates* those things in us. The more we make love, the more we'll *want* to make love, and the better we'll feel about ourselves and the whole act of lovemaking. Sex just makes life better.

Studies show that making love increases the levels of the chemicals in your brain. Specifically, the ones that make you want sex. So the best way to want sex more is to have it more. You've got to do it to want it.

The bottom line is that great sex doesn't just happen. A successful marriage doesn't come about by chance or luck of the draw. You have to *make* it happen. And you *can*. I'm convinced that each one of us can have a wonderful marriage and sex life if we will commit ourselves to the effort we know it will take. I encourage you to start making it happen today.

Praying for Yourself and Your Husband

A great sex life can't be built on determination and willpower alone. It takes one more crucial ingredient—prayer.

A friend of mine recently shared that sex is often frustrating for her. This young mother is easily distracted, finds it hard to get (and stay) aroused, and suffers from fatigue. She asked me what she could do to improve her sex life.

"I guess my biggest problem," she said, "is that I have no idea where to even start."

"Have you tried praying about it?" I asked her.

"Praying about sex? No, I never really thought about that. I pray about everything else, but it seems kind of weird to pray about sex."

Want to kick-start your sex life but don't know where to start? Start on your knees. Pour out your heart to God. Let Him know where you're at—and where you want to be. Admit that you have no clue how to get from point A to point B. Ask Him to take you there.

Every one of your needs is real and valid to God. Unlike us, He is not an eye-roller. He takes us seriously.

Where to Start

Where do I begin? How do I pray for my marriage and sex life? Let me suggest four prayer requests to get you started.

1. *Pray for your own relationship with God.* "If we aren't right with God, then we aren't going to be right with each other," my sister Bethany comments. "Repenting and asking for forgiveness from God and each other must occur before anything sexual."

2. *Pray for your husband's spiritual life and growth.* If your husband isn't saved, pray for his salvation—a shared belief system will take your sex life to a new level of intimacy.

3. *Pray for protection for your marriage.* "Prayer keeps us together and helps our focus," Bethany says. "It gives us a bond and connection that's hard to explain, but it's so strong and powerful."

   "I believe in the power of prayer," says my friend Jodie. "The enemy is out to destroy marriages and homes. It's critical that we take this seriously!"

   In *The Book of Romance,* author Tommy Nelson points out that Solomon's wife (Song of Songs) was always on the alert to the things that might harm her husband and interceded in prayer for him on a regular basis.

   "She was aware that her husband had enemies—both in the natural and in the spiritual realms—and she set herself to be his foremost lookout post."

4. *Pray for sexual desire, willingness, and energy to make maximum effort.* What if you don't feel comfortable asking

God to help you want sex more? Think of it this way, my friend. God made sex. He invented sex. He created sex. It was His idea. It is His design, His plan, His baby. He knows all about it, and within the context of marriage, He sees it as a beautiful expression of love.*

"I pray that I'll enjoy sex more," my friend Daphne says, "and God answers."

The "Mystery" of Prayer

Please don't ask me how prayer works when everything else seems to fail. Just chalk it up to God's sovereignty. He made the world, He knows how it works, and He's obviously in charge. And even though I've seen the power of prayer a gazillion times, I still doubt sometimes that it will really work *this* time...

For example, someone once told me that if you're struggling with feelings of jealousy, bitterness, anger, or hatred toward someone, you should 1) ask God to take the feelings away and 2) pray for that person—asking God for blessings to be poured out in his or her life.

Yeah, okay, sure. Any praying I do for *her* is going to involve heaping coals to be poured on her big, fat, lying head!

Well, I tried it once. After about a week of intense bitterness toward a certain individual, I decided to pray for her instead. At first, it was the hardest thing ever. But it gradually got easier. I prayed for her marriage, her kids, her health, and for blessings both financial and emotional. And, oh my word—it worked. The bitterness gradually slipped away.

Imagine applying this to your husband. If sex is a struggle, it might be because of pent-up feelings of bitterness or resentment toward your mate. When you pray for God's blessings to be poured out into your husband's life, your love for him will come easier.

God's philosophies about life seem so skewed to me sometimes. They're completely illogical (from what I can see), yet time and time again, they work! "The foolishness of God is wiser than man's wisdom," as 1 Corinthians 1 says.

If someone wrongs me, and robs me of my rightful peace and

---

* Again, I strongly encourage you to read Stormie Omartian's *The Power of a Praying Wife*. Stormie breaks down prayer for your husband into 30 components and offers lots of Scripture and sample prayers. If you're serious about praying extensively for your husband, this is an excellent book.

happiness, it only seems natural that bitterness and revenge are the keys to reclaiming what I've lost. Yet God has somehow worked it out so that bitterness does nothing more than further rob me of joy.

Harboring bitterness is like drinking a steaming cup of poison *yourself* and expecting your *enemy* to get sick. Who suffers when I'm bitter? Pretty much just me.

Joy and bitterness—like light and darkness—are incompatible roommates. You can't have them both at once.

Get Specific

What concerns about your sex life can you think of to take before the Lord? List specific prayer requests on an index card or in a journal. Pray through them daily—or even several times a day.

> *"Help me to enjoy the times he grabs my breasts and bottom while I'm making supper, instead of shooing him away."*

> *"Help me to think of creative and genuine ways to compliment my husband in bed. I don't want it to be awkward or sound stupid."*

> *"Help me not to be grossed out by giving my husband oral sex, because I know how much he loves it."*

> *"Help me to concentrate on sex tonight and forget about the kids, the bills, and tomorrow's hectic schedule."*

> *"Please help me not to be afraid to give myself completely to my husband and not think self-conscious thoughts about my body."*

> *"Help me not to give up on orgasm without first giving it my best shot. I want to have one!"*

I'm sure you can think of plenty more from your own personal experience.

We often don't have because we don't ask. God isn't going to be embarrassed or offended by any of these (or other) requests. He wants you to be explicit, to communicate specific things you need and want from Him.

Two Steps Back...

I'd give anything to be able to proudly report to you that after writing this book (and faithfully putting all of my own brilliant advice into practice) that my sex life is off-the-charts fabulous, my husband and I feel madly in love, and life is only getting better with each passing day.

But alas, it is only partially true. First of all, I have failed miserably when it comes to consistently following my own advice. My pesky, selfish little sin nature is always poking her head out of that hole in the ground where I tried to bury her.

I've found that a good sex life often takes one step forward, two steps back. Or a giant leap forward and three or four tiny steps back. I'm always losing bits and pieces of the ground I overconfidently thought I'd permanently gained.

One night a few months ago, Gabe wanted to make love and I was in a foul mood. I tried to blame it on my pregnancy, but that excuse was getting old fast.

"I'm done with sex!" I blurted out. "I've had it!"

He could sense that I wasn't serious, just a bit overhormonal, so he didn't take my harsh words too personally.

"Okay, but what about your book?" he wanted to know. (Of course, this one was what he was referring to.)

"Forget the book! I'm not doing it!" And I meant it. Sort of. Honestly, I hadn't touched my manuscript in two weeks—I knew better. Conviction would have stuck her fingers in her ears and waggled her annoying little tongue at me the minute I started flipping through these pages.

All that is to say, prayer got me back on track. I faced the music— namely the song whose words go,

> *I need God in my sex life—*
> *I can't wing it on my own.*
> (Not a real song, by the way.)

And I soon remembered something I'd forgotten—life is better when you're having sex with your husband on a regular basis.

Where Are You Headed? How Are You Getting There?

I have slowly figured out that God rarely lets me conquer any significant struggle completely. He allows me to take steps in the right direction but keeps me from ultimate lasting success. It's too important to Him that I keep turning to Him and trusting Him, rather than myself. Thankfully, He's the God of second chances. With Him, I always get another opportunity to do things right. His grace and compassion are new every morning. He's the God of fresh starts.

Paul writes in Galatians that "only crazy people would think they could complete by their own efforts what was begun by God."* That hits home for this crazy girl. How about you?

A little later, he asks us to answer a provocative question:

> Does the God who lavishly provides you with his own presence, his Holy Spirit, working things in your lives you could never do for yourselves, does he do these things because of your strenuous moral striving or because you trust him to do them in you?

Ouch. I'm starting to get the point. All the strenuous moral striving in the world can't guarantee a great marriage.

Paul then adds that anyone trying to "live by his own effort, independent of God, is doomed to failure."

Life isn't about reaching a point where I'm finally self-sufficient in every key area—finances, marriage, parenting, career, sex, relationships. Life is about learning how to handle mistakes and failures when they come. Learning how to rely on God in the midst of messy, often painful, circumstances. Realizing that self-sufficiency isn't even a desirable goal. A mutual reliance on our spouses, rooted in a dependency on God and a growing relationship with Him, is.

When we belong to Christ, our sinful nature has been crucified, put to death. Since we've chosen this life, a life controlled by the Holy Spirit, Paul exhorts us to "make sure that we do not just hold it as an idea in our heads or a sentiment in our hearts, but work out its implications in every detail of our lives."

My prayer is that you will work out God's will for your marriage in every detail of every day.

---

* The following four Scripture quotations are Galatians 3:3; 3:5; 3:10; and 5:25. All are taken from *The Message* paraphrase.

A Final—and
Honest—Word

Way back at the beginning of this book, I mentioned that one of the reasons I wrote it was to give my sex life a much-needed boost.

What's the verdict? Did it work? Was the venture a success?

Yes and no.

If success means that I was transformed into a perpetually sensual creature who constantly craves all varieties of sex and has the hottest marriage bed around, then—um, no, I didn't quite achieve my goal. Not even close.

But if I measure success by the overall atmosphere of my marriage, my improved attitude of love (with accompanying actions) toward my husband, and our more frequent "wows" in the bedroom, then yeah, I was pretty successful.

I say "overall" because if I focus on isolated disappointments or setbacks, I might get discouraged.

Consider the events of my last few days. Seventy-two hours ago, I was glowing. Everything was perfect. Sex was stellar. I felt loved, cherished, wanted.

A few hours later, Gabe and I had a conversation that crushed me. He said something I took to be a slam on my personality, the essence of who I am. *How can I make love to him ever again?* I thought.

Less than an hour later, I was over it. All was forgiven.

Forty-eight hours ago, I was stressed out over some finishing touches on this book. Gabe suggested that some real-life sex might fuel my imagination. My first thought was—*I don't have time for that!* Then I decided it couldn't hurt. And again, I hate for there to be huge discrepancies between my books and my life.

He was right. A little lovemaking was just what I needed. Wow.

Twenty-four hours ago, I was rushing around like a madwoman, doing laundry, washing dishes, paying bills...

One hour ago, Gabe's request for some lovin' caught me by surprise. *Three nights in a row? Are you going for Guinness here?* I couldn't seem to focus, and it wasn't one of our better moments.

Twenty-four hours from now...who knows?

The only thing I can say with certainty is that I will keep at it. I'll keep taking steps in the right direction, I'll keep working on my attitude, I'll keep trying to shove selfishness aside, and I'll keep asking my heavenly Father for help.

A good marriage and sex life can definitely get easier to maintain over time, but it will never become completely effortless. There will always be ups and downs. Like all of life's truly best things, it's not free.

I don't know where you're at in your marriage. I do know that if you're struggling, you can't just pray a quick prayer and poof!—great sex life! But you can definitely take steps *right now* to get things moving in the right direction.

God has a vision for my marriage—and for yours. A wonderful, beautiful plan that involves unfathomable intimacy with our husbands—spiritual, emotional, and sexual.

No, it's not always easy. Yes, it takes hard work and sacrifice. But I have found that, when I fall on my knees and offer my marriage and sex life up to the Lord, I have opened the doors for a lifetime of fulfillment.

Resources and References

Arp, David and Claudia. *No Time for Sex*. West Monroe, LA: Howard Publishing Co., 1997.

Craker, Lorilee. *We Should Do This More Often*. Colorado Springs, CO: Waterbrook Press, 2005.

Dillow, Linda, and Lorraine Pintus. *Intimate Issues*. Colorado Springs, CO: Waterbrook Press, 1999.

Farrel, Bill and Pam. *Red-Hot Monogamy*. Eugene, OR: Harvest House Publishers, 2006.

Feldhahn, Shaunti. *For Women Only*. Sisters, OR: Multnomah Publishers, 2004.

Gardner, Tim Alan. *Sacred Sex*. Colorado Springs, CO: Waterbrook Press, 2002.

Gregoire, Sheila Wray. *Honey, I Don't Have a Headache Tonight*. Grand Rapids, MI: Kregel Publications, 2004.

LaHaye, Tim and Beverly. *The Act of Marriage*, updated ed. Grand Rapids, MI: Zondervan, 1998.

Leman, Kevin. *Sheet Music*. Wheaton, IL: Tyndale House, 2003.

Linamen, Karen Scalf. *Pillow Talk*. Grand Rapids, MI: Revell, 1996.

Nelson, Tommy. *The Book of Romance*. Nashville: Thomas Nelson, 1998.

Omartian, Stormie. *The Power of a Praying Wife*. Eugene, OR: Harvest House Publishers, 1997.

Penner, Clifford and Joyce. *The Gift of Sex*, rev. ed. Nashville: W Publishing, 2003.

Rosenau, Douglas E. *A Celebration of Sex*. Nashville: Nelson, 2002.

Schlessinger, Laura. *The Proper Care and Feeding of Husbands*. New York: Harper Collins Publishers, 2004.

Wheat, Ed and Gaye. *Intended for Pleasure*, third ed. Grand Rapids, MI: Revell, 1997.

Other people's marriages look perfect.
Yours doesn't.
And you've only been married 27 days!

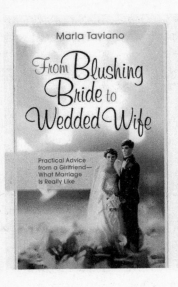

For years, you dreamed about meeting Mr. Right, and finally you found him. Next came romantic dates, then a beautiful wedding, and now... *reality!*

Is married life a little different than you thought it would be—or maybe a lot different? Do you wonder if something is wrong, if other people feel the same way about their new marriages? Are you sometimes intimidated by wives who seem to have it all together?

Marla Taviano has been there. Married only eight years, she knows what it's like to adjust from unrealistic expectations to real life. With tons of humor and the sensitivity of someone who's been in your shoes, she offers hope and encouragement as she demonstrates how you can...

- realize that you're *Mrs.* Right—for him
- fight fairly—and smartly
- get along with your in-laws
- keep the romance sizzling
- smooth the path to a great future together

Relax. You're not alone. You too can experience God's plan for your marriage and make a successful transition *From Blushing Bride to Wedded Wife.*

Harvest House helps you find the road to a more fulfilling marriage

The Power of a Praying® Wife
Stormie Omartian

Worrying about your marriage changes nothing...Praying about it can change everything. Stormie Omartian shares how God has strengthened her own marriage since she began to pray for her husband concerning key areas in his life. Every woman who desires a closer relationship with her husband will appreciate this refreshing look at the power of prayer in marriage.

Becoming the Woman of His Dreams
Sharon Jaynes

Do you want to become the woman of your husband's dreams? The woman who makes him sorry to leave in the morning and eager to come home at night? If you would like a little "wow!" back in your relationship with the man you married, *Becoming the Woman of His Dreams* offers you an insightful look at the wonderful, unique, and God-ordained role only you have in your husband's life.

> *"Sharon has captured the essence of a man's core needs and offers practical steps women can take to be the woman of his dreams."*
> Dennis Rainey, president of FamilyLife

Saying It So He'll Listen
Dr. David Hawkins

In his 25 years of private practice, psychologist David Hawkins has helped hundreds of women get their message through to their man.

- Find out how you can come together and work on problems as a team.

- Learn to identify problems and experience real change in your relationship.

- Discover ways that you can enjoy deeper intimacy and more joy.

The "Seven Cs of Communication" will revolutionize the way you relate to each other as you learn to speak more calmly, clearly, and compassionately.

What a Husband Needs from His Wife
Melanie Chitwood

What's the very best thing you can do for your relationship with your husband? It's to focus on your walk with God and let Him transform you—and your marriage. Melanie Chitwood shows you how to

- find true fulfillment and identity apart from possessions or activities
- enjoy greater companionship and intimacy
- survive and even thrive in relationally stormy times
- renew the passion and romance in your marriage

Other good books to help you enjoy a passionate life together

Red-Hot Monogamy
Bill and Pam Farrel

Did you know that the best sexual experiences are enjoyed by married couples? Marriage and relationship experts Bill and Pam Farrel reveal what you need to know to add spark and sizzle to your love life. You'll discover how

- God specifically designed you to give and receive pleasure from your mate
- a little skill turns marriage into red-hot monogamy
- sex works best emotionally, physically, and physiologically

Along with ways to create intimacy when you're just too tired and how to avoid the "pleasure thieves," this book offers hundreds more ideas to inspire romance and passion in every aspect of your lives together.

Romancing Your Husband
Debra White Smith

Debra reveals how you can create a union others only dream about. From making Jesus an active part of your marriage to arranging fantastic romantic interludes, you'll discover how to "knock your husband's socks off"; become a *lover-wife*, not a *mother-wife*; and ultimately, cultivate a sacred romance with God.

Experience fulfillment through romancing your husband...and don't be surprised when he romances you back!